MANAGING DIVERSITY IN AN EQUAL OPPORTUNITY WORKPLACE

A Primer For Today's Manager

Lorence L. Kessler

National Foundation for the Study
of Employment Policy
1990

FOREWORD

A manager who surveys today's workplace is likely to see a labor force that is significantly more diverse than that encountered by managers in the recent past. Current trends in demographics indicate this diversity will continue to grow. In the coming decade, the new entrants to the labor force will reflect steady increases in the percentage of women, Black Americans, Hispanic Americans, Asian Americans, and immigrants moving into the workplace. At the same time, managers in a broad variety of industries are finding themselves pressed by competition to achieve and maintain higher levels of quality in the production and delivery of goods and services.

In this environment, the companies that are most successful in managing workplace diversity will have a distinct advantage over those that try to ignore the demographic changes. In addition to the implications for employment policies, these changes present the challenge of a more diverse population of customers in this country. Thus, the terms "managing diversity" and "valuing diversity" are heard with increasing frequency as businesses seek to develop strategies for dealing with these changes.

In the search for effective and innovative approaches, one specific issue has remained somewhat murky. That is, how does the concept of managing diversity relate to the requirements of our existing laws on equal employment opportunity and affirmative action? For some, the focus on managing diversity is seen as simply another way of approaching traditional EEO concerns. For others, the concepts of managing diversity and affirmative action are viewed as entirely separate issues. Yet others have suggested that managing or valuing diversity is a dramatic new step that goes beyond what they see as the limited horizons of equal opportunity requirements.

The purpose of this monograph is to examine the relationship between the major concepts of diversity management and the traditional concept of equal employment opportunity embodied in our civil rights laws. Without attempting to take on the many aspects of the diversity issue that have been, and will continue to be, the subject of scholarly research by sociologists, anthropologists and psychologists, this book focuses on the subject from the perspective of the principles of equal employment opportunity. It begins with the premise that those principles should be — indeed, must be — regarded as representing a legitimate and practical approach to dealing with workplace diversity. The monograph's purpose is not to endorse or criticize any of the specific approaches to diversity management offered by the various experts in this field. Rather, it is intended to provide managers and policy makers with a discussion to raise some of the questions that will need to be addressed as diversity management theories and programs are put into practice.

The research for this monograph included interviews with dozens of people from different companies. The Foundation gratefully acknowledges the extensive assistance received from these employers in this project. To present the range of their different views as accurately as possible, the various perspectives and ideas conveyed during those conversations have been incorporated into a series of fictional dialogues that accompany the text. The dialogue format permits a broader perspective on the issues of general interest, while avoiding the need to attribute particular statements to individuals from specific companies. For those who wish to read about programs undertaken by particular companies, the Resources section lists a number of articles on this topic which discuss such programs in a company-specific manner.

The points raised in the dialogues are discussed in the accompanying text and commentary written by Lorence Kessler, an attorney with a Washington, D.C., law firm who specializes in equal employment opportunity law and who advises the Affirmative Action Practices Committee of the Equal Employment Advisory Council. By presenting the issues in this format, it is hoped that the monograph will be a useful handbook for managers and those individuals within a company responsible for designing and implementing diversity management initiatives.

June 1990   Edward E. Potter
Washington, D.C.

ABOUT THE FOUNDATION

The National Foundation for the Study of Employment Policy is an educational foundation formed in 1983 under Section 501(c)(3) of the Internal Revenue Code. Since its inception, the role of the Foundation has been to assist policymakers and the public in understanding the practical implications of employment policies being formulated by the courts, governmental agencies and legislative bodies and the impact that such policies have on the ability of U.S. companies to compete in the global marketplace.

The Foundation also serves as a research and educational resource for the Equal Employment Advisory Council (EEAC) and the Labor Policy Association (LPA). EEAC is a non-profit association composed of more than 210 companies dedicated to the establishment of nondiscriminatory employment practices. LPA is a non-profit association of corporate employee relations executives of more than 140 of the nation's leading businesses which monitors the development of employment policies at the federal level.

The Foundation has published numerous monographs and policy papers on a wide variety of employment policy issues including affirmative action, drug and alcohol abuse, immigration reform, and employee selection. For example, its recent monograph, *Winning the War on Drugs: The Role of Workplace Testing* (1989), addresses the legal and scientific issues relating to drug testing in the workplace and recommends the establishment of minimum federal standards. It has had a significant impact on the public policy debate on this important social issue.

vii

In the past several years, the Foundation also has developed a series of training programs that have been well-received by employers. These include training programs on the basic equal employment opportunity laws, affirmative action planning, effective handling of EEO charges, and the "Equity at Work" training program for supervisors and managers.

A list of the Foundation's monographs, policy papers, and training publications can be found at the back of this book.

TABLE OF CONTENTS

CHAPTER I

OVERVIEW

Today's manager is challenged by competitive pressures to maintain and achieve the highest levels of quality in the production of goods and services. This challenge, in turn, demands greater effectiveness in managing the company's workforce — its critical human resources. Increasingly, as the shortcomings of our educational system become evident and as the demand for job skills escalates, managers cannot take for granted their ability to attract and retain the skilled workers they need. To a greater extent than in the recent past, a company's ability to compete in its industry is linked closely to how well it can respond to the question: "Where are we going to find the people we need to get the work done?"

As employers reach out to attract skilled individuals from all segments of our society, managers are finding themselves with the challenge of bringing together into an effective team a workforce of people from different backgrounds. The history of this country, of course, is one that demonstrates the positive results that can be achieved by successfully bringing together people from different backgrounds. On the other hand, a number of recent incidents remind us that in a multicultural society racial and ethnic tensions and discrimination can be very real problems. Demographic trends indicate that, in the years ahead, our society generally will be faced with the challenge of realizing the positive potential represented by a diverse population while avoiding or over-coming the potential for tension and discrimination. Nowhere will this challenge be more immediate than in the workplace. Indeed, the workplace will be one of the primary points of continuing interaction for people from all segments of our society.

Of course, ethnic and racial differences are not the only differences in background one finds in today's workplace. The increasing number of women in jobs once held primarily by men also contributes to workplace diversity, as does the increasing reliance on older workers and workers with disabilities.

For a manager, the challenge presented by such differences can be stated simply: Managers increasingly will be called upon to work effectively with individuals who are different from themselves. To attract and retain individuals with the skills necessary to do the required work, managers will need to create a workplace environment that comfortably accepts and respects people's *differences.* To fashion this diverse workforce into a productive team, the manager will have to create an environment that appreciates and builds upon individual strengths. At the same time, it will be incumbent for the manager of a diverse workforce to foster a spirit of inclusiveness that seeks to emphasize the common ground and common interests that flow from *individual similarities.*

Meeting this challenge will require managers to develop and exercise a broad range of so-called "people skills." Perhaps none of these skills will be more important than a sensitivity to individual differences and a working appreciation of the principles reflected in our nation's equal opportunity laws. To the extent that a manager has successfully conveyed to employees the fact that an individual's race, sex or ethnic background will not be a factor in employment decisions, that manager will be in a better position to resolve many of the issues that are likely to arise in a diverse workforce. In a workplace where the commitment to equal opportunity has not been successfully communicated, a manager may find that otherwise simple workplace issues become unnecessarily complicated because they also involve concerns about potential or perceived discrimination.

This monograph begins with a discussion of the basic reasons why companies have seen the need to focus resources on diversity management. This chapter outlines some of the elements found in most company programs responding to workplace diversity. Chapter II examines the basic principles underlying the nation's equal employment opportunity laws, with a view toward the general relationship between these laws and the efforts to manage a diverse workforce. Chapter III explores the important role that company programs to enhance quality can play in creating the common goals and the common ground that are so critical in bringing individuals of different backgrounds together as a workplace team. Chapter IV explores the similarities and differences between traditional affirmative action efforts and the newer initiatives to manage workplace diversity. Next follows a discussion of how the law deals with individual differences in the workplace, and the important concerns that underscore the need to avoid stereotyping of individuals. Subsequent chapters discuss the process of responding to workplace diversity, beginning with an assessment of the existing corporate culture and suggesting some of the questions that must be asked and answered in that process. Chapter VIII examines the use of employee organizations and support groups, and some of the legal issues which arise in the creation of such groups. Finally, the paper discusses some specific situations in which employers have responded with a positive approach to diversity management, building upon the basic principles expressed in the civil rights laws.

Defining the Terms

To examine the relationship between workplace diversity and equality of opportunity, it is helpful to begin with some basic definitions. The concept of *equality of opportunity,* of course, reflects the spirit of our civil rights laws that prohibit employment discrimination on the basis of characteristics such as race, sex, color, national origin, religion, age or disability. It is important to recognize, however, that this concept is something broader than a narrow set of prohibitions. While the laws were written with a focus on prohibiting discrimination against individuals in certain protected classes, the practical results of those laws in many, many workplaces has been the development of practices, procedures and standards designed to assure fairness for *all* employees, regardless of whether they are members of a protected class.

The concept of workplace diversity has a similar quality in that, if managed well, it can have a positive impact that extends beyond a narrowly-defined class of individuals. *Diversity* can refer to any or all of the various characteristics that may make one individual different from another. In its most narrow sense, it includes differences such as race, national origin and gender. It also can include differences in characteristics such as age, or religion, or the fact that a

- 4 -

person has a disability. These characteristics serve as the starting point for many discussions of workplace diversity. But, the concept need not be so limited. Indeed, one of the fundamental aspects of this issue is the recognition that the principles of managing workplace diversity can lend themselves to a much broader definition of "diversity."[1]

Equality of opportunity will produce a workforce that generally reflects the demographic profile of the pool from which workers are drawn. *Diversity management* represents the skills and policies necessary to bring the variety of individuals in that workforce together as a productive team.

The Need To Address Workplace Diversity

Among most of the employers interviewed for this monograph, there is general agreement as to the basic *reasons* that have served as catalysts for undertaking initiatives to address workplace diversity. First, demographic trends reflected in birth rates and the average age of workers in this country indicate that we are heading into an era marked by labor market shortages. For the first time in nearly fifty years, there will be more jobs than workers. And, the shortage of workers will be compounded by the fact that most of the new jobs being created in our economy have skill

---

[1]Thus some of the companies designing initiatives in this area have chosen to think of diversity as something which goes beyond those characteristics that are already the subject of federal EEO laws. They have developed concepts of diversity that also encompass differences in characteristics such as marital status, parental responsibilities, sexual orientation, physical appearance, personality, and others.

requirements that demand training beyond high school.[2]
Second, businesses are recognizing that quality performance
can be a significant competitive edge in markets at home and
overseas. Both of these factors place a premium on being
able to attract and retain workers who have the skills to do
the job, and mean a competitive disadvantage for the
employer who does not tap all the sources of available talent.
Similarly disadvantaged is the employer who accumulates
unnecessary turnover costs because skilled individuals find
that another employer provides a workplace environment
that is more accommodating to their individual needs.

To meet these challenges, managers are finding it is to
their advantage to promote an "inclusive" rather than an
"exclusive" approach to the individual differences reflected in
the workplace. This has been the driving force behind the
various initiatives on diversity management.

To some extent, the issues related to diversity are
reminiscent of issues that have arisen in the past when our
labor market brought together individuals of different
nationalities and ethnic backgrounds. But diversity also
encompasses many new questions. For example, new issues
are evolving as the workplace demands that men and women,

---

[2]*See* statements by Senator Edward Kennedy and Secretary of Labor
Elizabeth Dole in Hearings before the U.S. Senate Committee on Labor
and Human Resources, January 26-27, 1989. Senator Kennedy noted that
the "skills gap" will make "employment impossible for some citizens and
expensive for employers." Observing that American business is already
spending billions of dollars a year just to bring workers up to a level of
skill that society once assumed would be achieved through public
education, Senator Kennedy pointed out that, "As the labor shortage
intensifies, as schools continue their decline, and as jobs that emerge in
the future become increasingly technical, these costs will accelerate."

as well as the old and the young, work together in roles quite different than in the past. Finally, the emphasis on diversity is also a reflection of the increasingly international character of many companies, as they do business in world-wide markets.

Typical Elements of Diversity Programs

In responding to workplace diversity, companies have explored a broad variety of approaches. What is at once fascinating and frustrating is that in examining the programs and initiatives within various companies, one does not find unanimity about any aspect of these programs — even their ultimate goals. Indeed, not all firms even use the "diversity" label to describe their efforts. But, it is possible to point to some general similarities. For many employers, the first step in examining the "diversity" issue is the appointment of a committee or task force to study the situation, to identify the potential issues, and to explore potential responses. Typically, the most common elements found in the initiatives to address workplace diversity have been the following:

1. Candid Assessment of Workplace Practices and Culture

Generally, this involves examinations or audits of the existing employment practices and the workplace culture. The purpose of such investigation and analysis is to discover those policies or practices that may be undermining the goals of (a) attracting and retaining skilled workers, and (b) providing a workplace in which each of those workers is encouraged to perform to his or her full potential. Typically, the result of such audits has been the adoption of new policies, or the modification of existing policies, to respond to or to accommodate the needs of individuals.

2. Enhancement of Communications

This includes: (a) communications from employees to management, to help management better understand the attitudes and concerns of employees; (b) communications from management to employees, to assure that employees know their responsibilities, their performance standards, and the rules (written and unwritten) by which the workplace functions; and (c) communications among employees, particularly those from different backgrounds.

3. Increased Awareness and Sensitivity

This includes efforts to provide managers, and employees generally, with a broader knowledge of the differences among people and greater sensitivity to how those differences can be accommodated in the workplace without any negative impact on workplace performance. The most effective approaches in this regard seem to be those that do not focus solely on differences. Ultimately, the goal is to bring people together by promoting an appreciation that these real differences need not mask the values and characteristics shared by all of the individuals in that workplace.

The emphasis placed on any of these elements can differ from one company to another. Indeed, how the issue of diversity confronts a particular organization, or individuals within that organization, may differ significantly. For the managers of a fast-food restaurant chain that is dependent on a steady supply of entry-level service workers, changes in the labor force are already apparent. These managers are already confronting the challenges of managing a very diverse group of employees. They are recognizing that they must reach out to groups of individuals who traditionally may not have been thought of as being in the labor pool for such jobs.[3] For other managers, who require highly-trained specialists such as engineers or scientists, the scarcity of talent may already be apparent, but the diversity in the labor market may not yet be so obvious. Even for these managers, however, the changing nature of the workforce will be felt as they realize the importance of retaining the skilled workers they already have, and avoiding the recruitment, training and development expenses generated by unnecessary turnover.[4]

Enhanced Management Skills

In considering the numerous challenges listed above that today's manager must respond to, it is reasonable to ask just what types of skills a manager must develop to be effective in a diverse workforce.

Among the corporate managers who were interviewed in the preparation of this book, there was a strong belief that most of the skills required to manage a diverse workforce are skills that have been long recognized as good management

---

[3]See, for example, *For Retarded, Independence in Real Jobs,* New York Times, January 2, 1990, at A1; *Great Number of Older Americans Seen Ready to Work,* Wall Street Journal, January 26, 1990, at B1.

[4]See, for example, *Changing America: The New Face of Science and Engineering,* the Final Report of the National Task Force on Women, Minorities, and the Handicapped in Science and Technology (December 1989), indicating that our nation faces a serious shortfall of scientists and engineers and that blacks and Hispanics together comprise only 4 percent of all employed scientists and engineers.

practices, including the important quality of being sensitive to individual differences.[5] Managing a diverse workforce does not necessarily mean developing a different set of management practices. It does mean that managers are going to have to exercise a higher level of skill in using those traditional good management techniques. It means a manager will need to have a better sense of his or her own personal style of management and be able to deal effectively with the tendency to use stereotypes to short circuit the process of getting to know about the individuals with whom he or she works. Finally, it also means developing an awareness of the numerous ways that one individual can be different from another and an understanding that one can appreciate those differences while building on the many similarities that can be found among individuals.

In helping to develop this combination of awareness and management skills, some companies have set up separate training sessions — using some of the resources listed at the end of this paper — on workplace diversity issues. Others have chosen to incorporate the training on workplace diversity into the regular management skills training sessions held for supervisors and managers. Either approach can be successful. Indeed, as the discussion in the following chapters highlights, the key to success in any aspect of a diversity management program is not how well a company follows a particular formula, but rather how well the company assesses and responds to its own specific situation and needs.

---

[5]There are a variety of noted texts that describe these traditional skills in detail. Several of these are listed in the Resources section at the back of this book. In addition, the essential principles of management are succinctly summarized in Peter Drucker's discussion of management as a liberal art in *The New Realities* 228-231 (1989).

CHAPTER II

DIVERSITY AND EQUALITY OF OPPORTUNITY

Wes, Lydia and Mark are all employees of a large United States corporation known as Megatech. It is now after 4:30 p.m., and they are leaving a meeting at corporate head-quarters related to the consolidation of several facilities recently acquired by the company.

Wes, who has been with the company about 20 years, is a division manager. **Lydia,** an attorney who specializes in employment law, has been with the general counsel's office at Megatech since her graduation from law school about 15 years ago. **Mark,** who joined the company within the past year after graduating from business school, has been working on the consolidation project. They each have more work to do before leaving for the day. But, finding themselves in the midst of a conversation about several of the issues brought up at the meeting, they decide to stop in the snack bar and continue their discussion.

Wes: You know, it is going to be a real challenge to integrate these new facilities into our operation. From a business point of view, the acquisition makes sense. But, there's going to be some culture clash, on management style and any number of other issues.

Lydia: I gathered from the meeting that the people you are assigning to the new facilities are some of your best managers.

Wes: They are, all right. But, trying to mesh two cultures can be a tricky chore for anyone.

Lydia: I'm learning that myself lately. I'm on the task force to examine cultural diversity at Megatech. We want to come up with some approaches for improving our managers' awareness of the diversity in our workforce, and for improving their ability to manage that diversity.

Wes: That's a real challenge. You know, on the way home each day, I pass two neighborhoods that have taken on entirely new ethnic identities in the last ten years. But, still, I was amazed when I heard the workforce projections. More immigration; increasing numbers of women working; and, more black, Hispanic, and Asian Americans.

Mark: It's probably time to come up with a better word than "minority."

Lydia: That's for sure. I've never particularly liked that term anyway. I wouldn't be sorry to see it go. Whatever word we use, though, a lot of the problem issues are still going to be the same.

Mark: What approach is the task force going to suggest?

Lydia: Well, you heard the approach we are using to integrate the newly-acquired facilities?

Mark: You mean the idea of drawing together the best of

each culture, stressing that each individual has something to contribute? Our basic "Valuing People" approach?

Lydia: That's right. We want to stress the upside potential of getting everyone on the team, regardless of differences in race, sex, or ethnic background.

Wes: May I make a suggestion?

Lydia: Sure. We need ideas.

Wes: When you put this initiative together, keep in mind those folks of mine out there in the regions who are going to have to sell this idea, and implement it. Give me something I can use to bring everyone on board, including that fellow who says: "What about those of us who aren't part of any 'different culture'? What about those of us who aren't part of any minority group? What's the company doing for us?"

Lydia: The fact is, the company needs everyone's skills.

Wes: Well, I hope that will be emphasized. I'm always bewildered by some of those attitude surveys — you may see them, too. Many younger white males wonder if there are opportunities for them, because they believe the opportunities all go to other people. And yet, a lot of women and black men feel there are no opportunities for them either, because all of the opportunities are going to white males.

Lydia: I think a positive approach to diversity management can respond to those feelings, and the fears they reflect. A management philosophy that focuses on the job you do, not on any of the individual characteristics that may make you different from your neighbor, can be a positive message for *all* employees.

Wes: So then, how does this relate to our EEO programs?

Lydia: That's a question that needs to be thought out very carefully. Our task force has some different ideas on that. But, the fact remains that discrimination — because of race, because of ethnic background, because of sex — still has an impact in our society. And the EEO laws are still in place. I wouldn't want to see anyone get a message that our commitment to EEO is anything less than it has been.

Mark: But with labor shortages, it will be senseless for people to discriminate.

Lydia: Discrimination has never made sense, but that hasn't made it easy to eliminate. And, in the past, whenever our country has had people coming into the labor force who were different from those already present, the situation generally has been ripe for discrimination.

Mark: I'll tell you how I see it. The idea that you have to treat everyone exactly the same doesn't always make sense in the real world. People are different. We all recognize that. Isn't it time we admitted it out loud, and started moving beyond EEO?

Lydia: That's the million dollar question. I haven't tried to work it out from a legal point of view. But, personally, I don't think we ever move *beyond* EEO. This company always has believed in taking some initiatives that go beyond the minimum that the law requires. And, I think that's what we are doing with diversity management. But moving in that direction doesn't mean leaving EEO behind. In fact, with the changing demographics, it's probably going to be more important than ever that we make our EEO principles a fundamental part of each effort we undertake.

Mark: Oh, I don't mean to say EEO isn't important. But, as you just said, Megatech is a good company on EEO matters. It's always listed as one of the better places for women and blacks to work. And, if you talk numbers, our numbers are pretty good. Now that we have brought this diverse mixture of people into the company, we ought to be trying to tap that diversity. And, I don't think we can do that by continuing to say to our managers: "Pretend that everyone is the same."

Lydia: I hear you. But, remember our reputation on EEO doesn't get us any privileges under the law. That reputation doesn't mean we can't be challenged by *any* individual who thinks he or she was denied an equal opportunity.

Wes: So, you're saying we need to be very careful whenever we start thinking of ourselves as so successful that we have outgrown the basic concept of EEO.

Lydia: Yes. But, I think the emphasis on diversity management is critical, too. Just look at what we're saying when we talk about changing demographics. We are going to have thousands and thousands of people coming into the workplace who are — in race, or ethnic background, or culture, whatever — different from the group that currently holds the largest share of the jobs, and a majority of the positions of authority. What's more, the people coming into the workplace will be *different from one another.* They will come from a variety of different groups or cultures. People who do not routinely interact with members of other groups are going to find themselves required to interact in the workplace with people from very different backgrounds.

Wes: That's a good point. If we don't manage this well, we could have plenty of problems.

Lydia: Both productivity problems and legal problems.

Mark: Sure. But, honestly, from a legal standpoint, doesn't our reputation as a good employer make it easy to defend ourselves?

Lydia: The reputation is nice, Mark. But it won't carry us very far if we use policies that result in different treatment for people from different racial or ethnic backgrounds. You see, it's very difficult to *prove* that you don't discriminate. But, what you can show is that you have a set of policies and procedures that you apply the same way to everyone, regardless of their race, sex, or ethnic background. And this company has done a good job of instituting those kinds of procedures. That's what can make this a good company to defend. Speaking of that, I'd better get back to the pile of work on my desk.

With that, Wes, Lydia and Mark wind up their chat and head back to their offices, agreeing to exchange suggestions about the diversity task force.

Commentary

The fact that Wes, Lydia and Mark each see the diversity issue somewhat differently is no surprise. Employers at the leading edge of this issue report that some of the strongest disagreements about the goal of their diversity initiatives, and about the course they should take, occurred among those on the diversity task force. Indeed, it probably would be an unhealthy sign if the issue evoked no differences of opinion.

1. Labor Force Trends

Wes, Lydia and Mark are correct, of course, about the nation's changing population. As has been well-documented in the Department of Labor's *Workforce 2000* study and elsewhere, the changing population is going to have significant effects on the face of the American workforce in the years ahead.[6] The major trends are summarized below.

Preliminary projections indicate that the 1990 Census will show that during the 1980's, we added nearly 23 million people to the population. About one-fifth of that growth was the result of adding 500,000 legal migrants each year, with Mexicans, Filipinos, Chinese, Koreans, and Vietnamese being the most common newcomers. As a result, the 1990 population will be approximately 84 percent white, 12 percent black, 3 percent Asian or other races, and 8 percent Hispanic.[7]

---

[6]W. Johnston and A. Packer, *Workforce 2000: Work and Workers for the Twenty-First Century*, Hudson Institute (1987). *See also*, R. E. Kutscher, *Outlook 2000: Projections Summary and Emerging Issues*, Monthly Labor Review, November 1989, at 66-74.

[7]This compares to our 1980 population which was 86 percent white, 12 percent black, 2 percent Asian or other races, and 6 percent Hispanic. *See* J. Waldrop and T. Exter, *What The 1990 Census Will Show*, American Demographics, January 1990, at 25. In these statistics, persons of Hispanic origin may be of any race.

The growth of the labor force in the United States will be at the slowest rate of any period since the 1930's, reflecting a similarly slow rate of growth in our population generally. As the baby boom generation heads into middle age, the average age of workers will increase, reflecting the smaller supply of younger workers.[8]   Women will constitute an increasing percentage of the workforce, concentrated primarily in some "traditionally female" occupations but also with increased representation in those jobs formerly thought of as "traditionally male."[9]   Minorities will also increase their representation in the labor market, reflecting the fact that both black and Hispanic populations in this country have grown more rapidly than has the white population.[10]   In

---

[8]By the year 2000, the median age for employed Americans will reach 39 years; in 1987, the median age of workers was 36. *Workforce 2000* at 79-81. Today there are more than 30 million Americans over the age of 65 — approximately 12 percent of the population — and this segment of the population is increasing by nearly six million every decade. In fact, in the last two decades, the over- 65 age group has grown more than twice as fast as the rest of the population. K. Dychtwald and J. Flower, *Age Wave: The Challenges and Opportunities of an Aging America* 6-8 (1989).

[9]The movement of increasing numbers of women into the American workforce has been characterized by scholars as one of the most significant developments of the 20th Century. By the year 2000, approximately 47 percent of the workforce will be women, and 61 percent of all women in the United States will be employed. In 1960, only 19 percent of all mothers with children aged six or under held jobs outside the home. By 1985, that number had increased to 52 percent, with the trend expected to continue through the end of the century. *Workforce 2000* at 85.

[10]This increase in the black and Hispanic populations is attributed to both immigration and birth rates higher than the white population. Black, Hispanic and Asian Americans will make up a large share of the net

addition, there will be more immigration than at any time since World War I.[11]

What then will be the profile of the United States labor force in the year 2000? Projections indicate that white, non-Hispanics will account for approximately 74 percent of the labor force, compared with 79 percent in 1988. While white participation in the labor force is expected to grow at the same rate as the overall labor force, that growth will be slower than the increased growth for blacks, Asians and others, and Hispanics. Blacks will comprise approximately 12 percent of the labor force in the year 2000, compared with 11 percent in 1988. By the year 2000, Asians and others (including American Indians, Alaskan Natives, and Pacific Islanders) will comprise 4 percent of the labor force, compared with 3 percent in 1988. And, by the year 2000, Hispanics will comprise 10 percent of the labor force, compared with 7 percent in 1988. Women will constitute 47

---

expansion of the labor force. The group comprising the largest share of the projected increase in the non-white labor force will be black women, who will outnumber black men in the workforce. *Workforce 2000* at 89.

[11]The immigrants who entered this country in the 1970's reflect a wide variety of educational backgrounds, a trend which is expected to continue through the year 2000. While 22 percent of those immigrants were college graduates, many more had only a modest formal education. In fact, 25 percent of the immigrants had less than five years of school, compared to only three percent of native-born Americans. K. Hopkins and W. Johnston, *Opportunity 2000: Creative Affirmative Action Strategies for a Changing Workforce* 10, U.S. Department of Labor (1988).

percent of the labor force in the year 2000, compared with 45 percent in 1988.[12]

The impact of the changing demographics, of course, is not limited to the workplace. The new faces in the workforce also represent consumers. Already, manufacturers are recognizing and responding to the increased number of dollars controlled by women who are working and playing a significant role — if not the primary role — in supporting a family.[13] Firms are also recognizing the markets represented by black, Hispanic and Asian Americans. For firms that choose not to address diversity in some manner as a workplace issue, the reality of new markets may nonetheless force them to focus on understanding cultural differences and how to communicate across those differences.

The years ahead represent a significant opportunity to increase the job opportunities for those who have been

---

[12]*See* H. N. Fullerton, Jr., *Outlook 2000: New Labor Force Projections,* Monthly Labor Review, November 1989, at 9-10. It may be noted that projections about the movement of workers into and out of the labor force indicate that the profile of workers leaving is much different than the profile of workers entering. For example, white, non-Hispanic men make up one-third of the projected labor force entrants but almost one-half of the projected leavers.

[13]This trend in the nature of family households is also of interest to employers. Preliminary projections indicate that the 1990 Census will show that during the 1980's the number of households headed by married couples increased by approximately 3.8 million, while there was an increase of 2.9 million in the number of family households headed by a woman with no husband present, and an increase of more than 500,000 in family households headed by a man with no wife present. *See* J. Waldrop and T. Exter, *What the 1990 Census Will Show,* American Demographics, January 1990, at 27.

excluded in the past. But, equally important is the stubborn fact that the years ahead are going to produce more and more jobs that will demand a higher level of skills. This means there will not automatically be opportunities for everyone; but there will be opportunities for those who have the needed skills.[14] Current statistics about our educational system, however, indicate that our schools are not doing as good a job as they must in providing these needed skills. The weaknesses of the education system, when compared to schools in other countries, have been documented in a variety of studies.[15]

The impact of these educational shortcoming is reflected by the low rate of high school completion by blacks and Hispanics during the 1970's and 1980's. If this continues, it will eliminate significant numbers of the young people in those communities — not only from jobs requiring some college education — but also from those rapidly growing job opportunities in the technical areas that require some training beyond high school. Or, to put it another way, if

---

[14]The same data that produce the workforce projections for the year 2000 also reveal that today blacks and Hispanics are overrepresented in industries that are losing jobs and underrepresented in the most rapidly growing occupations. See R.E. Kutscher, *Outlook 2000: Projections Summary and Emerging Issues,* Monthly Labor Review, November 1989, at 67. See also the discussion of educational issues in *The Decade of the Hispanic: A Sobering Economic Retrospective,* The Policy Analysis Center, National Council of La Raza (December 1989).

[15]*See, for example, Investing in People: Strategy to Address America's Workforce Crisis,* issued in September 1989 by the Secretary of Labor's Commission on Workforce Quality and Labor Market Efficiency. *See also, A Nation at Risk: The Imperative For Educational Reform,* The National Commission on Excellence in Education, U.S. Department of Education (April 1983).

these educational trends continue, it will mean the sectors of our population that are the fastest-growing components of our labor force will not be getting the basic education they need to take advantage of the job opportunities our economy is expected to produce in the years ahead. While these problems have significant implications for our society generally, they also pose special challenges to employers competing to attract those individuals who do have the needed skills.

Finally, these trends should not be assessed in a vacuum. Rather, they should be viewed in context of the other changes faced by business today and in the years ahead. Most companies are confronting an increasingly competitive market, and most are responding with the knowledge that, to be successful, they must maintain high levels of quality and efficiency in producing the goods or services they take to that market. To serve the overall needs of the corporation, a diversity program must be compatible with — and ideally, strongly supportive of — these other ongoing corporate goals.

2. Practical Legal Issues

As a follow-up to Lydia's comments, it may be noted that while the emphasis of our EEO laws is on equality of treatment as a way of assuring equality of opportunity, it is not accurate to characterize those laws as being premised on a belief that all people are the same.[16] Rather, the premise

---

[16]The primary equal employment law in the country, and the focus of most of the legal discussion in this paper, is Title VII of the Civil Rights Act of 1964. Passed as a result of the civil rights movement of late 1950's and early 1960's, Title VII prohibits discrimination on the basis of race,

of our EEO laws is simply that employment decisions can and should be made without considering factors such as a person's race, color, sex, national origin, religion, or age.

In theory, so long as a company's employment decisions are made without regard to those characteristics, the employer may base decisions on any legitimate business reason it chooses. In practice, however, the issue is not so simple. If one of the employment decisions made by the company is challenged, then some impartial fact-finder (such as a federal judge) must decide whether or not the company illegally discriminated. In defending itself in such a case, the company is obviously in a much stronger position if it can point to a set of rational, regularly-followed, business-related criteria that are used as a basis for making selection decisions.

By way of an example, imagine yourself as the judge in a case challenging an employer's decision to discipline an individual because of excessive absenteeism. The employee asserts that the real reason for the discipline was his race. If the employer can show that its treatment of the employee was consistent with a standard policy that the company follows in *all* cases — regardless of the race of the employee involved — you probably would conclude that the company's decision in this particular instance was not racially motivated. On the other hand, suppose the company simply states that

---

sex, national origin, religion or color. Title VII is enforced by the federal Equal Employment Opportunity Commission. The EEO laws also include the Age Discrimination in Employment Act (ADEA), passed in 1967, and the prohibitions on discrimination against a person because of a disability found in the Rehabilitation Act of 1973 as well as the Americans with Disabilities Act of 1990.

race was not a factor and then tells you that it just "does what seems right in each case." What basis would you have for ruling in favor of the company? What if the company tells you that it has no set standards for determining what constitutes excessive absenteeism or what disciplinary action is appropriate in such cases? You might find it much harder to accept the company's claim that race played no part in this particular decision.

Thus, the EEO laws themselves do not dictate that everyone is to be treated the same. Rather, the importance of similarity of treatment flows from the nature of the burdens placed on employers in employment discrimination cases. To defend their practices, employers — as a practical matter — must be prepared to demonstrate the routine consistency and predictability of those practices.

There has been a great deal of litigation about the burden of proof in employment discrimination cases; that is, what an individual must prove to the court to support his or her charge of discrimination and what an employer must be prepared to prove in order to defend itself. But no matter how the burdens of proof are technically defined by the courts, employers know that, as a practical matter, to avoid liability they must always be prepared to explain and justify any differences in their treatment of members of different protected groups. To the extent that this burden is increased by new legislation or court decisions, of course, employers will find it all the more necessary to cling to the security of a "treat everyone the same" approach.

Finally, it should be noted that Lydia was entirely correct in her observation that a "good" reputation in the area of equal opportunity earns a company no special privileges under the law. A good reputation can be helpful, both in reducing the likelihood that charges will be filed and in corroborating other evidence that an employer acted with legitimate motives. But in the final analysis, any company, regardless of its reputation, can be challenged on virtually any employment decision, and the company must, therefore, be prepared to defend those decisions.

In many cases, challenges to a company's employment policies are framed in statistical terms. Consequently, it is important to understand the way numbers are used in equal opportunity cases.

Statistics showing that an employer has fewer women or minorities in its workforce than would be expected — based on a comparison with the EEO profile of the relevant labor pool — can provide the basis for a charge of discrimination. But, the fact that women or minorities are well represented in an employer's workforce does not provide an automatic defense to a charge by an individual who claims to have been discriminated against on the basis of race or sex. Proof that an employer has not discriminated against an entire class does not prove that it did not discriminate against a particular individual. To defend itself, the employer cannot simply point to its "good numbers." Rather, the employer must point out a legitimate business reason behind the decision being challenged as discriminatory.[17] Again, as a practical matter, the employer's ability to provide a satisfactory explanation is typically much stronger if the employer has followed a standard policy that it applies in the same way to everyone.

---

[17]*See Furnco Construction Corp. v. Waters*, 438 U.S. 567 (1978).

In discussions of the relationship between diversity management and equal employment opportunity, those who suggest the EEO laws serve only a very limited purpose often proceed from the assumption that while such laws can force the removal of "Whites Only" signs from an organization's door, they do little to promote full acceptance of minorities within the power structure of that organization. It can be argued that this is not a fair characterization of the impact that the EEO and affirmative action requirements have had, and will continue to have, in the workplace. What is most important, however, is to recognize that there is a significant overlap between these two concepts to the extent that the ultimate goal is to promote full utilization of society's human resources throughout the company.

CHAPTER III

ASSESSING THE NEED FOR A DIVERSITY INITIATIVE AS PART OF QUALITY MANAGEMENT

As noted earlier, a diversity management program should be more than just compatible with other, ongoing corporate goals. Ideally, it should be instrumental in helping to achieve other goals that depend on effective use of human resources. The following dialogue illustrates some thoughts on how this potential for synergy with other programs — such as efforts to enhance quality — may be highlighted as a way of gaining broader management support for a diversity initiative. The importance of achieving increased quality in production can be one of the key elements in creating a common goal for the individuals in a diverse workforce.

Lydia is having lunch with a group that includes two men who direct business divisions within Megatech. **Philip,** who has been with the company for more than 20 years, gained his reputation for innovative management when he turned around one of the company's major product lines. He now is generally regarded to be on a fast track headed for even higher levels of responsibility. **Gene,** also a senior manager, has advanced steadily through a variety of sales and marketing positions during his 17 years with the company.

In the course of their discussion, Lydia mentions the diversity initiative and her need to sort out some of the issues involved. Both men respond positively, indicating it is an issue that has already caught their attention.

Philip: The changes you're talking about — in the supply of workers, and particularly in the supply of skilled workers — are critical issues in our efforts to remain competitive. When we do our strategic planning, we sometimes tend to take human resources for granted. If we are going to talk about where we want our company to be in five years, or ten years, we need to be asking whether we now have the human capital available to get us there. If we do, we need to consider what has to be done to keep those people. If we don't, we need to consider where and how we are going to find those people and attract them to our door. I hope your effort focuses on the critical business issues involved, and doesn't end up sounding like — pardon me — just another human resources program.

Lydia: I hope so too. We need to get the attention of managers. One key will be to have people like you involved. Employees need to see that there is interest and involvement from people at the highest levels. If this effort involves only human resources folks, it's going to be hard to convince others that it's a broad initiative.

And, once people begin to understand the changing demographics, I think they'll see that this issue is closely related to their ability to manage productively.

Gene: But, Lydia, you need to keep in mind that there are limits on the impact those workforce projections can have. Some people haven't heard about the projections, of course. But, for those of us who have read them, or heard presentations about them, the initial impact of the projections has begun to diminish.

Lydia: The projections are sound, though. The changes are coming.

Gene: Oh, I don't doubt that. But it's a message that's already been delivered to many of our managers. My impression is that they respond with interest, as we would expect. But then, a month later, they are up to their ears with problems they see as "today's problems." In that environment, projections about what our workforce will look like in eight or ten years become "tomorrow's problem" that never gets attention today.

Lydia: So, we need to add an element of currency or immediacy to the issue.

Gene: That would certainly help. If the weather report says we'll be getting snow next winter, it isn't going to attract much attention, even though it's an accurate prediction. But, if the report is that we'll be getting a bad storm in the next 24 hours, everyone pays attention. If you want people's attention, you need to be able to focus on something that's happening now. That's true even if what's happening now is only a small part of a much larger change that's occurring over the long term.

Philip: And, carrying your analogy a bit further, I think we want to avoid the position of the weather forecaster who predicts a major storm that never materializes. There are departments in our company where most of the employees are people with advanced degrees in engineering. The managers in those departments are not about to see the broad range of "diversity" reflected in the overall workforce projections. If we get a manager's attention only by predicting major demographic changes that the manager is not likely to see today, or anytime in the near future, the diversity initiative could lose credibility very quickly.

Gene: I think the answer — or at least one answer — may be to focus on what many managers are already seeing. To the manager, however, changes in the workforce generally occur one person at a time. We lose a lot of our immediacy impact if we allow the diversity initiative to be sold as a series of strategies that managers *may* need at some time in the future when most of their employees are women, or minority men, or individuals from other countries. The fact is that "diversity" management can become an issue the very *first* time a manager has to deal with someone who's different from himself.

Lydia: So, in this engineering department we've been talking about, we can bring home the "diversity" issue by stressing some of the changes that have occurred already.

Philip: That's right. The changes don't have to be dramatic. If that department used to be 100% white males and it now includes several women, one or two blacks, or a few individuals from other countries, that manager needs to be aware of how to deal with individual differences.

Lydia: But, my friends, how do I get the manager to believe that it's important to be responsive to such a small degree of diversity? The nice feature of the overall workforce projections is that they're compelling in that they suggest substantial changes. Our manager in the engineering department is likely to believe that such small changes are not enough to suggest a re-examination of management practices.

Philip: That's where our quality and competitiveness issues merge with our labor supply issues. The Chairman has made it very clear that he's serious about increasing our quality of production, and decreasing our tolerance for errors. A manager who is being pushed by this focus on quality — in fact, any manager who is seriously pushed by the need to remain competitive in a world market — is going to find that he cannot write off that part of his workforce that is "different."

Gene: The manager is going to have a greater stake in assuring that *each individual* can produce at the desired level of quality. So, your appeal to the manager is that some time spent on diversity management skills can pay a dividend in terms of the department's overall production. And maybe reduced turnover, as well. I think that kind of an approach can get people's attention because it promises the type of results a manager can understand.

Lydia: And, that approach will have obvious appeal to those managers in other departments who already are confronted with a workforce that reflects many different backgrounds.

Gene: The significant tie between "diversity" and "quality" I see is in the need for the company, or the manager, to spell out clearly what is expected from an employee. The quality initiative has forced us to re-examine a number of jobs and responsibilities that we used to define only in a very broad manner. Now, in many of those jobs, we have established certain quantitative goals to measure how well those jobs or responsibilities are carried out. The goals provide a basis of measurement that allows these jobs to be included in our push for increased quality and reduced errors. One of the things that the manager of a diverse workforce needs to confront is explaining to employees — in a way they can understand — exactly what is expected of them. These quality goals are certainly going to help that process.

Philip: I think that's critical, Gene. One of the things we noticed when we began developing the quality initiative was that, in the past, we had often pursued quality or excellence on the job by simply exhorting employees to, "Give it the old college try!" Or, "Do the best job you can." Those are great slogans, but they assume that everyone has an understanding of what is to be done.

Gene: And, unfortunately, there are too many situations where managers fail to articulate clearly what they expect. In a workplace where everyone has a similar background, and where there are few if any social or cultural barriers to overcome, this failure by the manager may not be a significant problem. In that setting, new employees can easily learn the rules and responsibilities from some of the other employees. But, in a more diverse workplace, that kind of informal communication may be less likely to occur, and less efficient when it does.

Lydia: I guess the same is true for some of the so-called "unwritten" rules that every workplace seems to have.

Gene: Absolutely. I can remember when I first started here, the people in my department were all very friendly — up to a certain point. I was the only black, and while no one seemed to exclude me from anything deliberately, no one was going out of their way to include me either. I think it was the same kind of discomfort anyone feels when he's new in a group that has been working together for a while. The difference, I think, is that, because of my race, it took some people a lot longer to become comfortable with me. The result was, it took me longer than some others to develop a real understanding of how the office worked, what the boss liked, and what he didn't like.

Once I understood the phenomenon, I was able to compensate for it somewhat. And, frankly, since becoming a manager, I've tried to keep that experience in mind. I think it's important to communicate with employees so they have a clear sense of what the boss expects. Now, I know that's not a new management concept. When it comes to a diverse workforce, though, the lesson may be that managers will need to put more skill and effort into such communications. We just can't assume that the correct messages will be conveyed through indirect or informal channels.

Lydia: The link between the quality initiative and the diversity initiative is interesting. But, you know, there is a legal consideration, as well.

Philip: I had a feeling you would say that, counselor. What line have we crossed now?

Lydia: Oh, it's not that. Actually, this is something that may make life easier for the legal department. As you may know, we're constantly worrying about how we can defend the use of subjective criteria for making selection decisions.

Philip: By subjective criteria, you mean something like "leadership ability"?

Lydia: Yes, in contrast to the number of units produced, the number of orders filled, or some other factor that can be measured quantitatively.

Philip: I thought subjective criteria were legal, as long as they aren't used to discriminate.

Lydia: That's true. We can defend our right to use them. But we've been advising the divisions that where they use subjective criteria, there should be some guidelines to explain what is meant by those criteria. We're trying to prevent situations where it might appear to an unsuccessful candidate that our "subjective criteria" are so broad or undefined as to permit intentional discrimination on the basis of race or sex.

I am much more comfortable, though, when there is some objective criterion that demonstrates an individual's performance. So, to the extent we can re-examine job responsibilities and find objective standards that accurately measure how well a person is performing the job, we will be making it easier for us to defend our decisions if they are ever challenged.

Gene: So, undefined or uncommunicated subjective performance standards are an enemy of both quality assurance and diversity management. To the extent we can replace such standards with clearly-communicated criteria, there's another bonus. We'll also be making our lawyers happy.

Lydia: I think you've got it.

Commentary

While the *Workforce 2000* projections have been a catalyst for the increasing focus on successful management of a diverse workforce, a variety of companies have found that the workforce projections may not themselves be enough to sustain a continuing diversity initiative. To the extent the initiative can be structured to highlight to managers that effective diversity management can help them achieve better overall management, the more successful the initiative is likely to be.

The quality programs in major companies have been identified with a variety of titles. Fundamentally, however, these programs are structured to push all aspects of the company to higher levels of quality and to reduce the tolerance for errors or mistakes.

1. The Push for Quality

Companies today increasingly see a commitment to quality as a significant element in maintaining their competitiveness. Achieving the desired level of quality demands something more than a simple check for defects at the end of a process. Rather, quality must be built into the process. The connection between quality in production and human resources is relatively basic, as reflected in the Secretary of Labor's Workforce Quality project:

> High quality goods and services cannot be produced unless there is a high quality work-force working with a high quality production process; and a high quality workforce can only be maintained when there is a high quality of working life.[18]

---

[18]*See,* M. J. Smith, F. C. Sainfort, P. C. Sainfort, and C. Fung, *Efforts To Solve Quality Problems* 7, Background Monograph No. 36 for

The push for quality in American industry is reflected by the Malcolm Baldridge National Quality Award, established by an Act of Congress in 1987 to promote quality awareness and recognize quality achievements of companies in the United States. The criteria for the award place an emphasis not simply on quality achievements, but on development of management systems for quality improvement. Among the seven categories examined in determining the award recipients is "Human Resource Utilization," which looks at the "success of the company's efforts to utilize the full potential of the work force for quality." Also examined are: "Quality Assurance," meaning the effectiveness of the company's systems for assuring quality control of all operations; and "Quality Assurance Results," meaning the company's results in quality achievement and quality improvement, demonstrated through *quantitative measures.*

Corporate efforts to assure quality, and to measure the results of quality improvement programs, have gone hand-in-hand with the development of refined equipment that allows the measurement of performance to a degree that may not have been possible a decade ago. These extend to measurements of both production quality and customer satisfaction. Obviously, some responsibilities within a company lend themselves to statistical measurements of quality more easily than others. But, to the extent that such assessments are practical as part of a quality assurance program, they can also serve as a useful tool for managers in a diverse workforce.

Investing in People, a report by U.S. Department of Labor Commission on Workforce Quality and Labor Market Efficiency (1989).

This ability to focus attention on precisely how performance is to be measured and to set standards that can be understood by both the manager and the employee, will be an asset to the manager who is dealing with a diverse group of workers. This type of understanding can cut through the social or cultural barriers that might otherwise allow an employee and manager to think they understand one another only to find out later that they have been consistently misinterpreting one another in terms of job performance.

Where performance cannot be reduced to easily understood objective criteria, the manager will have the task of taking steps to assure that the job responsibilities are clearly communicated. As noted, this has always been considered fundamental to good personnel management. But, it has not always been carried out. Often managers who failed to communicate were shielded from problems because the mono-cultural nature of the workplace made it easy for a new employee to learn — through an informal, on-the-job education — whatever was necessary. This same type of informal learning may well take place in some multi-cultural workplaces, but a good manager cannot depend solely on such uncertain channels.

2. Performance Standards: Subjective and Objective

As Lydia noted, an employer is not prohibited from using subjective criteria in making selection decisions. Indeed, such criteria are often necessary, particularly in performance appraisals. Those performance appraisals are often the most critical pieces of evidence in lawsuits challenging a discharge or a denial of promotion. In such cases, the employer can be asked to explain its subjective criteria in much the same way it is asked to explain the impact of its various objective standards.[19]

The potential for such challenges to an employer's subjective decision-making process means that the employer should be prepared to defend itself by offering evidence to indicate that the subjectivity is not "undisciplined." Similarly, when the Department of Labor investigates a government contractor's selection procedures for potential discrimination, special attention is given to subjective criteria and what guidelines the employer has issued to assure that managers do not use those criteria as a mask for discrimination against women and minorities.

Obviously, subjective criteria cannot be eliminated. But, the dynamics of a workforce that includes people from diverse backgrounds will dictate that employers place new emphasis on developing job descriptions and performance

---

[19]The Supreme Court has ruled that the disparate impact theory of discrimination, which focuses on the potential discriminatory effect of selection standards that are not discriminatory on their face, applies to subjective as well as objective employment standards:

> It is true, to be sure, that an employer's policy of leaving promotion decisions to the unchecked discretion of lower level supervisors should itself raise no inference of discriminatory conduct . . . .It does not follow, however, that the particular supervisors to whom this discretion is delegated always act without discriminatory intent.

Watson v. Fort Worth Bank and Trust, 108 S. Ct. 2777, 2786 (1988). Justice O'Connor noted that the "problem of subconscious stereotypes and prejudices" is one reason why courts must permit the impact of such subjective discretion to be examined. *Id.*

standards that can be clearly communicated. Where subjective criteria are employed, additional efforts may be necessary to promote a clear definition and a common understanding of the meaning of those criteria. Where modern technology makes it possible to produce new objective criteria, such as quantitative measures of production and production quality, employers are likely to find those measures useful not only as a tool to enhance quality but also as a tool to promote commonly understood standards of performance among workers from diverse backgrounds.

Among the employers interviewed for this paper, there was near unanimity in the belief that the ability to use "good business reasons" to justify the focus on diversity had been a key element in whatever success the diversity efforts had achieved. The strong connection between quality production processes and effective diversity management provides that business justification. In addition, a focus on quality production provides the enlightened manager with the common goal that can be so important in bringing a group of diverse individuals together as a working team.

CHAPTER IV

DIVERSITY MANAGEMENT AND AFFIRMATIVE ACTION

As part of its diversity management project, the company has brought a selected group of employees together to get their views about the company, its culture, and how its culture currently accepts or excludes individuals of different backgrounds. Following the session, several attendees remain in the room informally continuing the discussion begun during the session. In the group are: **Lydia,** the attorney whom we met earlier; **Gene,** the senior executive whom we also met earlier; **Nelson,** a 24-year-old customer service representative who has been with the company for two years since graduating from a liberal arts college with a sociology degree; **Maria,** a 30-year old who has held an accounting position with the company for nearly seven years; and **Paul,** a 48-year-old sales executive who has been with the company for nearly twenty years.

Nelson: I really appreciated the chance to be part of this session. Thanks for including me. I see this as a very positive step. I'm glad to see the company putting emphasis in this area.

Paul: It was interesting, all right. And, I think its exciting. But, I bet you I can predict the question I'm going to get when I mention this to some of the guys I work with. "What about those of us who aren't part of any different culture? Is this more affirmative action? Or is there something in this for everyone?"

Gene: You're a salesman, Paul. You know that how you describe something can have a big impact. Affirmative action is something that has not always been talked about in a positive tone. Diversity management may be an approach that can help us explain that our human resources management systems are geared to all employees, not just those who are members of certain racial or ethnic groups.

Lydia: We always have a difficult time describing that issue. But, the fact is there are some pretty strict conditions that must be in place before an employer can voluntarily use race or sex as a basis for giving a person preferential treatment. For the most part, affirmative action requirements are forms of outreach and recruitment, trying to enrich the pool of qualified applicants from which we make our selection.

Gene: You know that, Lydia; and I know that. But, the truth is there are a whole lot of employees who do not understand that. Many people think of "affirmative action" as a system of preferences or quotas. Some of my best friends are white — no kidding — and they've recounted numerous instances where they have heard white employees, or more specifically, white male employees, say "What's in this for me?"

Lydia: That's not a fair thing for them to be asking. Don't they know about the history of discrimination? Don't they see the relatively small number of minorities in upper level management jobs?

Gene: Perhaps they see that, perhaps they don't. What I'm afraid is more important is that — regardless of what they see around them — when they hear the term affirmative action, and even when they hear EEO, they think of it in a negative context, a "numbers game" that offers nothing for them.

Paul: Well, you heard the comments today from one of the younger white males in the group — that the company doesn't really offer him much of a future prospect because he's not part of any protected group, and because there have been lots of jobs eliminated by workforce restructuring.

Gene: We need to be prepared to counter that fear. Even though his fear is without any basis — I mean, we are going to need all the skilled people we can get. But sometimes I think we need to do a better job of dealing with that fear. And, frankly, that is one of the exciting aspects of the diversity management project. It doesn't have to carry the "zero-sum" message that some people incorrectly read into affirmative action. And yet, most if not all of the things we are doing in the name of affirmative action have a place in diversity management.

Maria: Well, can you answer one more question, please? I liked what I heard today. I like that the company is going to try to help employees work together better. And, that the company wants to promote awareness of some of the different cultures. But, there are still problems. I mean, I'm Latino. There are still a lot of people in my community who aren't getting the education they need to find good jobs. And, there are Latinos working here now who are never going to be able to advance unless there are some training programs available to them. What is going to happen? If we have cultural diversity instead of affirmative action, are we going to forget about the special problems that affirmative action was set up to deal with?

Gene: No. No. That's not going to happen.

Lydia: There are legal requirements, and — even if there weren't — our company is committed to continuing our affirmative action program.

Commentary

You don't have to be a legal scholar or a human resources manager to know that affirmative action is a controversial concept. Ever since it was first used in the 1960's, the phrase has meant different things to different people. For this reason, it is helpful to define exactly what the term means in the law.

1. Affirmative Action Requirements

The affirmative action requirements imposed on government contractors by the federal government focus on encouraging employer efforts to enrich the pool of individuals considered for employment opportunities. As part of this process, larger contractors are required to develop a written affirmative action plan that involves a detailed analysis of the employer's workforce and employment practices. The Department of Labor, which audits these affirmative action plans, has been careful to stress that to the extent a contractor is required to set goals as part of its plan, those goals are not "quotas." The contractor's compliance is based ultimately on whether the contractor has made "good faith efforts" to comply, not simply on whether numerical goals have been achieved.

There are situations where — as a remedy for past discrimination — a court will require an employer to hire individuals of a certain race or sex. The Supreme Court has allowed the use of preferences in some other circumstances. But, the situations where such preferences are legitimate are relatively limited. For example, an employer may treat gender or race as a "plus" in the selection process only where the job at issue is one where there is a manifest imbalance in the representation of women or minorities in traditionally segregated job categories;[20] and the preference may be exercised only where the person receiving the favorable treatment is *qualified* for the job.

Nonetheless, the issue of preferences — whether they are used and the extent to which they are used — remains one which is commonly misunderstood. Even if this misunderstanding cannot be corrected, a well-structured diversity management effort can promote an image of a company that is responsive to all of its employees.

At the same time, however, there is a natural relationship between the type of analysis expected as part of an affirmative action plan and the type of workplace assessment which has been used in some diversity management initiatives. Indeed, keeping in mind the strong business reasons underlying the desire for effective diversity management, it is interesting to recall that the federal affirmative action requirements themselves are based on business reasons.

---

[20]*See Johnson v. Transportation Agency, Santa Clara County, California,* 107 S.Ct. 1442, 1451-57 (1987).

That is, the federal government's affirmative action require- ments have not been applied to all employers in general, but rather have been tied to the awarding of government con- tracts. In examining those requirements, courts have suggested that the government's justification for imposing the affirmative action obligation was not simply because it was believed to be socially desirable. Rather, as one court noted:

> [The government] acted in the one area in which discrimination in employment was most likely to affect the cost and the progress of projects in which the federal government had both financial and completion interests. In direct procurement the federal government has a vital interest in assuring that the largest possible pool of qualified manpower be avail- able for the accomplishment of its projects.[21]

To translate this into the context of the workforce in the year 2000, an employer who tries to draw all of its human re- sources from the approximately 40 percent of the labor force who are white males will be at a significant disadvantage to

---

[21] *Contractors Association of Eastern Pennsylvania v. Secretary of Labor*, 442 F.2d 159, 171 (3d Cir.), *cert. denied,* 404 U.S. 854 (1971). In this case, the court noted that the origins of the non-discrimination requirements in the government contract compliance program go back to an order signed by President Roosevelt in 1941 "as a prerequisite to the successful conduct of our national defense production effort." *See* Executive Order 8802, signed June 25, 1941. The connection between non-discrimination and efficient production is seen as well in the law passed by Congress in December 1941 "to expedite the prosecution of the war effort." Among other things, that law provided the War and Navy Departments with the authority to require non-discrimination clauses in all war related contracts.

an employer who draws upon the resources offered by the entire labor force.

2. The Goals of a Diversity Program

Many companies, by virtue of their status as government contractors, already have an obligation to go "beyond EEO" in the sense that they are required to take affirmative action to assure equal employment opportunity. As noted, this program involves a detailed process of statistical analysis, including the requirement that statistical goals be set for job groups where women or individuals from minority groups appear to be underutilized. The goals required by the Department of Labor are to be tied to the availability of women or minorities in the relevant labor market.

What types of goals can be established for measuring the success of a company's diversity efforts? Can the same goal-setting process used in affirmative action planning be used as part of a diversity initiative? How are the affirmative action goals affected by the demographic trends indicating that the profile of the workforce is changing? Specifically, does the existence of a more diverse labor pool mean that an employer should be setting goals to achieve a workforce that reflects such diversity?

In answering this question for a particular company, it is necessary, of course, to have some sense of what is intended by the setting of numerical goals for hiring or promotion, and what kinds of pressures or incentives are placed on managers to meet those goals. Generally, however, the current law does not recognize the mere desire to achieve a diverse workforce as a legal justification for using race, sex or national origin as a positive factor in employment decisions to try to achieve that result. Thus, an employer should use extreme caution in setting any numerical goals for hiring or promotion as part of a diversity initiative that appear to be arbitrary or that cannot be shown to have some rational connection to the pool from which people are selected.[22]

---

[22]The Supreme Court addressed the issue of using racial preferences to maintain a diverse workforce in the case of *Wygant v. Jackson Board of Education,* 476 U.S. 267, 273-275 (1986). In that case, the school system sought during a layoff to maintain minority role models for its minority students by retaining minority teachers with less seniority while non-minority teachers with more seniority were let go.

The lower court had endorsed the "role model" rationale, but the Supreme Court rejected that approach, pointing out that the "role model" theory was based on the percentage of minority students in the school, rather than the percentage of minority teachers in the labor market. For this reason, the Supreme Court noted, there was no logical stopping point and no legitimate remedial purpose for the racial preferences sought to be justified under the "role model" approach.

In rejecting the "role model" theory, Justice Powell observed that if the Court were to endorse the idea that black students are better off with black teachers, the Court could be seen as contradicting the Court's landmark school desegregation decision holding that "separate but equal" schools are inherently unequal and thus unconstitutional. *See, Wygant,* 476 U.S. at 276, citing *Brown v. Board of Education,* 347 U.S. 483 (1954).

It may be noted, however, that Justice Stevens, in a dissenting opinion, supported the "role model" theory. Justice Stevens suggested that in the context of public education, a school board could reasonably conclude that an integrated faculty would be able to provide benefits to the student body that could not be provided by an all-white, or nearly all-white, faculty.

> For one of the most important lessons that the American public schools teach is that the diverse ethnic, cultural, and national backgrounds that have been brought together in our famous "melting pot" do not

On the other hand, as the labor pool from which an employer draws persons becomes more diverse, or becomes richer with minorities, it will be expected that an employer who is not discriminating will over time have a workforce that reflects that diversity. This is nothing more than the basic theory expressed by the Supreme Court in several early cases involving statistical proof of discrimination.[23]

To the extent a company wants to establish some other types of goals to motivate and to measure the success of diversity efforts, the experience of the employers interviewed for this project provides some creative approaches. These approaches focus on the importance of the link between a diversity initiative and sound business purposes. Thus, several companies have used these business purposes as the basis for setting different types of targets or goals. For example, a company's efforts to increase diversity awareness may be reflected by that company's success in attracting business from new segments of the marketplace. Or, goals based on the desire to reduce the extent of turnover in a

---

identify essential differences among the human beings that inhabit our land. It is one thing for a white child to be taught by a white teacher that color, like beauty, is only "skin deep"; it is far more convincing to experience that truth on a day-to-day basis during the routine, ongoing learning process.

476 U.S. at 315 (footnote omitted).

[23] See *International Brotherhood of Teamsters v. United States,* 431 U.S. 324, 339 n. 20 (1977), where the Court observed that "absent explanation, it is ordinarily to be expected that nondiscriminatory hiring practices will in time result in a work force more or less representative of the racial and ethnic composition of the population in the community from which employees are hired."

workforce, or to reduce the amount of turnover expenses, can measure the degree of success for some diversity management efforts.

3. Continuing Need for Affirmative Action Outreach Efforts

While there are many ways in which diversity management efforts and affirmative action efforts seem to complement one another, it must be pointed our that a focus on diversity management cannot entirely replace affirmative action efforts. Even as they were focused on planning diversity awareness efforts, the companies interviewed here were quick to point out that such efforts are not intended to reach all of the problems included under the umbrella of affirmative action. Indeed, just as the changing demographic trends highlight the need for a focus on managing diversity, some of those same trends highlight serious issues that are outside the diversity focus and yet need urgent attention. These are issues such as the education crisis that is having its most severe impact on minority youth in urban areas.[24] These problems, too, have implications for the future of our society, and solutions may well require employer efforts that go significantly beyond the initiatives undertaken as part of diversity awareness.

---

[24]For example, the action plan spelled out in *Changing America: The New Face of Science and Engineering,* the Final Report of the National Task Force on Women, Minorities, and the Handicapped in Science and Technology (December 1989) at 22, notes that, "Overwhelmingly, in schools in poverty areas, many Hispanic children receive an inadequate basic education, including poor instruction in mathematics and science. High school completion rates must be increased and early mathematical and science instruction must be improved to attract more Hispanic students to careers in science and engineering."

CHAPTER V

UNDERSTANDING DIFFERENCES

One of the most delicate issues surrounding the management of cultural diversity is the question of to what extent, if any, it is valid to regard differences among people as group-related characteristics. This question is likely to be discussed and debated in the course of any company's examination of diversity initiatives. Indeed, several of the companies interviewed for this paper reported that this question arose on numerous occasions as their diversity efforts proceeded. In an earlier chapter, we explored the basic relationship between diversity management and equal employment opportunity laws. In this chapter and the next, we focus specifically on the issue of dealing with differences in a manner that is consistent with the EEO laws.

To set the stage, and to get an appreciation for the manner in which this issue arises in company sessions, we join a discussion among three of our friends from Megatech: **Mark**, who has joined the company within the past year; **Lydia**, from the company's legal staff; and **Gene**, an executive who has been with the company for a number of years.

Mark: I have been giving this more thought since the first time we discussed it. I understand there is an important legal purpose behind the company's efforts to apply the same rules to every employee in every case. But, we know that virtually all of our managers are going to be exposed, more so than in the past, to people who come from backgrounds that are different from their own. Understanding those people, and getting the most out of them, is going to take an appreciation of some of these differences. The manager is going to have to recognize some of these differences. The idea of treating everyone the same simply will not work anymore.

Lydia: I agree, Mark. Certainly, there are changes coming. They are already here in many instances. There is truth in what you are saying. But, look at it another way.

If I imagine myself as someone who has recently arrived from another country, I'm not sure that the idea of being treated differently is going to be all that reassuring to me. I think I might tend to be suspicious of any process that didn't treat me like everyone else. In those shoes, I would be keenly aware of how hard it can be to understand the rules. But, in those shoes, it could also be very reassuring to know that there are rules, the *same* rules for everyone.

Gene: The situation for me has been somewhat different. When I was young, I saw discrimination — up close and personal, as they say. At times it was blatant and repulsive, and that's not something you forget. I wished for a society that would treat me just like everyone else, where my being black wouldn't matter. But, some people wouldn't, or couldn't, get past the race issue.

As I've gotten older, though, I've come to know another problem that can be very hard to deal with. That's when whites expect me to be just like them.

There are situations where I want the company to treat me just like anyone else. But, there are times when my being black — and having grown up in a black community — means that the situation I confront is, *in fact,* different, strictly because of my race. To figure out how to deal with such situations means recognizing and dealing with the race issue.

Lydia: I think I understand, Gene. But maybe an example would make it clearer.

Gene: Sure. When I first joined Megatech, I worked as a sales representative, just like most everyone else. And I confronted all of the sales problems that a salesman learns to deal with. There were people who didn't know about our product; people who liked our competitor's product and had to be convinced that ours was worth a try; people who had used our product in the past and, for some reason, had a bad experience that was still fresh in their memory. All of these situations were handled in our training.

But, for a significant number of the contacts I had, I was the first black salesman they had ever dealt with. They may have been used to seeing someone from our company, but they were not used to dealing with a black person. And, that situation had never been touched on in our sales training. Too few whites seem to appreciate that for a black person to survive, he or she has to develop a strategy for dealing with racial attitudes. That's something a white salesman does not need in his bag of tricks. But, it was something I had to use almost everyday.

Lydia: So it's in our interest as a company to see that any of our employees who are in that position can develop that strategy.

Gene: Absolutely. And, for this type of a situation, we don't have to have a different set of rules. I agree that we are all going to be better off with one set of rules — enlightened rules, I want to believe — that people can count on, rather than different sets of rules for different people. But, in the same way that we try to develop strengths on an individual basis and overcome problems on an individual basis, we should not be afraid to recognize certain "strengths" or "problems" just because they appear most often in individuals who come from a particular group.

Lydia: But, it seems very important that, ultimately, the company does deal with people as individuals, without assuming that they have certain problems to overcome, or that they possess certain strengths, because they are a member of a certain race or sex. We are not talking about immutable characteristics here. I always get nervous when someone notices a strength I have and then attributes it in some way to the fact that I am a woman. You know, "Nice job. What this needed was a woman's touch," or other comments like that.

Mark: But there are differences between men and women. Different strengths. Different styles.

Lydia: We need to keep the focus on *individual* strengths and *individual* styles. A person's style is influenced by his or her background. And a person's sex or race is part of that background — particularly in a society that often treats women differently from men, and blacks differently from whites. But these influences are not the same in every instance.

Gene: Once we start treating differences in style as immutable characteristics of one race or sex, we have laid the foundation for the very type of discrimination our laws are designed to prevent.

Lydia: That's so true. To say that women have a certain ability to deal with issues in a different way than men carries both positive and negative messages; it is difficult to deliver the first without providing a basis for inferring the second. Each time someone tells me my contribution added "a woman's touch," I wonder if they are not also saying that there are other qualities that could be contributed only by a man.

Gene: I agree. It makes me nervous when someone starts talking about recognizing that blacks are different from whites because some of those differences they may be putting on the list are differences that are primarily or directly the result of the discrimination we are trying to eliminate.

Mark: One of the suggestions I've heard uses a garden as an analogy. The garden has a variety of flowers. And each variety has slightly different needs in terms of water and cultivation. But each contributes to the overall beauty of the garden.

Gene: That's a pretty image. You need to be careful with that analogy, though, Mark. I think of myself as different from whites in some ways. But I know I'm different from some blacks in other ways. Not all blacks are alike; not all Latinos are alike.

Lydia: Not all whites are alike. So, our focus needs to be on individuals.

Gene: Right. Besides, the other problem that's out there, to a much greater degree than anyone has suggested, is that blacks and whites are still treated differently in too many situations. It's not usually intentional, mind you. Sometimes, it is done out of the desire to protect the black employee. But, when you come right down to it, it is a variety of discrimination that we need to focus more light on.

Mark: Do you mean here at Megatech, Gene?

Gene: Yes. I'm talking about those situations where a manager begins with a premise — perhaps without even articulating it to himself — that blacks are not as qualified as whites, or that women are inferior to men, in certain tasks or jobs. He doesn't refuse to work with the person, but over time he is much less demanding of his black or female employees. He may believe that if they were ever really tested they might fail. And, in the end, if the individual fails because of this lack of support, it only serves to reinforce the manager's original premise. This is a lack of management, and a lack of true mentoring.

Mark: Okay, that's a problem that needs attention. But, it seems to me, that there are certain differences that can be beneficial to us as a company. For example, women are often more keenly attuned than men to the needs and buying habits of other women. By employing women in key marketing positions, we can gain an edge over our competitors in selling products to women. It's often said that a person can't really know the needs of a given population if he or she is not a part of that population.

Lydia: Wait a minute. Think about what you are saying. Do you mean that there is a difference in the sexes that can be considered in making employment decisions? Can we say that a market analysis of products purchased primarily by women can be done better by a woman than by a man?

Mark: Sure. That's just common sense! And, it's time we start admitting it openly.

Lydia: I suppose that same common sense would dictate that, if we found that most of our products were purchased by whites, the market analysis could be done better by a white person than by a non-white? If I own a sporting goods shop, and I am hiring someone to sell golf clubs and equipment, would I be justified in choosing a middle-aged white male — rather than a black man or a woman — because I believe that most of my customers are going to be of a certain type?

Mark: No, I wouldn't go that far. That wouldn't be legal, would it?

Lydia: Certainly not. And neither is selecting a woman for a marketing position because we sell, or hope to sell, our product to women.

Mark: But, is anybody really going to object to us putting a woman in the market analysis position for those products?

Lydia: They may. If we get a sex discrimination claim from a male who was qualified for the job, we may as well start writing the check. But, more than that, once we start down that path of saying that women are better at certain things than men, or that blacks understand certain things because they are black, where do we stop? How are you going to respond to the next manager who says he has an opening for a supervisor and he thinks it's a job for a man?

Mark: That's different. Women can be supervisors as well as men. But, when we are talking about dealing with women's products, women are naturally better at understanding the market.

Lydia: But, Mark, it's not different. Once you start saying that women are naturally better at some things, you make it legitimate for people to argue that there are certain jobs that are women's jobs. That's been a major obstacle in our society for years, and it still is. We need to be breaking down, not building up, the idea that women are naturally suited for certain jobs. If we sanction that, then we also open the door for people to believe that men are naturally suited for certain other jobs. Don't you see? You're taking a giant step backwards.

Mark: Okay, maybe I am off base. I admit I don't understand all the legal stuff. But, I'm not trying to turn the clock back. I just have problems with any assumption that everyone is the same. People are not the same. We know that. Why doesn't the law let us admit it?

Lydia: The law does let you consider differences, Mark. The law permits — indeed encourages — you to look at the skills and knowledge that are required for a certain job and to make a decision on the basis of those skills.

Gene: So, there is nothing wrong with saying that we need someone in market analysis who is familiar with the needs and buying habits of women. No doubt, many of the people who have that skill and background will be women. But, there also are some men who have a lot of experience in that area. You see, we make the decision on the basis of the job skills possessed by the individual, not on the basis that this person is a member of a race or sex group that we assume has certain special skills or knowledge.

Mark: Aren't there going to be situations where a person's racial or ethnic background is going to be a factor? Let me give you an example. There has been a significant increase in the number of Vietnamese in our community during the past ten years. For a while, there were cultural problems that manifested themselves in any number of ways. There was a lack of communication, and probably a lack of trust, between various public officials and members of that community. In the past few years, however, the city's affirmative action and outreach efforts have led to the hiring of a Vietnamese as an officer on the police force. This has been a significant breakthrough in terms of communicating with that segment of the community. It has meant improvement in terms of routine police work and in communicating with the kids in the Vietnamese community about different recreation programs. Everyone has benefited.

Lydia: But, what do you think should happen when the Vietnamese officer is ready to be promoted to another position? Do you have to hire a Vietnamese to replace him?

Gene: I think you address the problem by looking to hire individuals who have the skills to communicate with various groups in the community. Certainly that would include those Vietnamese who can communicate with members of their community. But it would not foreclose someone with the same skills, who is not Vietnamese, from being considered for the position.

Mark: I'll give it more thought. But, I still think it limits us to not be candid about certain differences.

Lydia: Well, just keep in mind the legal limits. The law permits you to be candid in recognizing differences among individuals. What's more, the law forces you to recognize there are differences *among* women and there are differences *among* men. Where your marketing example offends the law is, it assumes that certain attributes or skills will be possessed *only* by women and not by *any* man.

Commentary

1. Communication and Awareness

Perhaps the best way for managers to increase their understanding of the people who make up the diverse workforce is to spend some time and effort getting to know more about *people generally,* as well as particular people from backgrounds different from their own. Indeed, it is not only managers who can benefit from such increased understanding. A number of employers have found there can be value in providing opportunities for such learning to employees generally.

But, to avoid some of the potential risks Gene mentioned, it is important to understand that this educational process is designed to increase the managers' awareness of the differences among people generally. And, from that increased awareness will come a perspective that gives the manager an increased ability to understand and work effectively with employees of different backgrounds. Ideally, then, the purpose of a session on Latin American culture would be to broaden the perspective of managers or employees who have never been exposed to that culture. The purpose would *not* be to train managers specifically on how to deal with individual employees who come from a Latin background. When it comes to dealing with employees, the focus of a manager in any workforce — whether diverse or homogeneous — must be on dealing with individuals.

At the same time, it cannot be assumed that talking about differences will come easily to all employees, or even to all managers. In environments where "race" is rarely mentioned, references to an individual's race or sex can have a high potential for creating ambiguity or misunderstanding. The individual may be uncertain whether the reference reflects a stereotype. For example, a manager's comment to a black employee that he has done a good job of fitting in and getting along with the predominantly white work group can put the employee in an awkward situation of not knowing whether the comment reflects bias and of wondering what kind of response is appropriate.

The difficulties that can arise when people feel it is acceptable to discuss "race" or "sex" are demonstrated in the situations which generated two recent cases decided by the Supreme Court. In one, an executive apparently advised a new employee — a black woman — that she might encounter some difficulty because she would be working with people who were not accustomed to working with blacks.[25] In another, several partners in an accounting firm, who were evaluating a woman accountant for partnership, wrote appraisal statements that reflected apparent sexual stereo-

_____

[25]*Patterson v. McLean Credit Union,* 109 S. Ct. 2363 (1989).

typing.[26] For example, it was suggested that she should dress more femininely and wear makeup.

While these are only two cases, they do serve to make the point that it should not be assumed that everyone in a management position fully understands the prohibitions of our existing EEO laws. If the purpose of advocating more discussion of race and sex differences is to promote sensitivity to the particular problems confronting women and minorities, it may be wise to carefully structure the sessions to prevent them from becoming nothing more than a forum for re-hashing old stereotypes and prejudices that may still be lingering in the minds of some individuals. Companies, as well as various experts, have differing views about how confrontational or adversarial these sessions should be. Clearly, if a confrontational approach is adopted, there should be opportunity for resolution before the session breaks up. The preferred approach is to give careful thought to the kinds of communication that you want to encourage, and then create opportunities for that communication to take place, without necessarily forcing it.[27]

---

[26]*Price Waterhouse v. Hopkins,* 109 S.Ct. 1775 (1989).

[27]One of the interesting questions that often arises during diversity awareness sessions is the practical matter of how to refer to the racial or ethnic background of particular individuals: "Black" or "African American?" "Hispanic" or "Latino"? While it may be appropriate to fall back on the designations used in various equal opportunity laws, it is important not to ignore the sensitivity of this issue. As EEOC Commissioner Evan Kemp has observed in explaining the movement away from the term "handicapped" toward the term "individual with disabilities" in the new Americans with Disabilities Act:

> As long as a group is ostracized or otherwise
> demeaned, whatever name is used to designate that

2. Dealing with Stereotypes: Old and New

Perhaps no trait is more human than the tendency to generalize on the basis of a few examples and then apply those generalizations in the future as we encounter new situations and new people. This tendency works in positive ways in the learning process. At the same time, it can be counterproductive — as well as illegal — for a manager to make generalizations about an individual because of what the manager may believe to be true about a group of which that individual is a member.

In most companies, once the subjects of managing diversity and respecting individual differences are raised, they are explored at great length. Initially, there may be some reluctance to talk about certain issues. But, eventually even the most sensitive issues tend to be raised. These include questions related to the real and imagined differences between individuals of different races or sexes.

The differences between men and women can provoke endless discussions, among men, among women, and in mixed company. Thus it is almost certain that these differences will

---

group will eventually take on a demeaning flavor and have to be replaced. The designation will keep changing every generation or so until the group is integrated into society.

W. Raspberry, *When 'Black' Becomes 'African American,'* Washington Post, January 4, 1989, at A19. A brief discussion of the political overtones attached to the terms used to designate Americans of African descent appears in K. Crenshaw, *Race, Reform, and Retrenchment: Transformation and Legitimation in Antidiscrimination Law,* 101 Harvard Law Review 1331 n.2 (1988).

be part of any sustained discussion of the increasing diversity of the workforce. Fortunately, we are not without guidance in this area. Virtually all of the real differences between men and women, and many of the perceived differences, have been addressed by the courts in the context of sex discrimination lawsuits. Most often, these cases have involved challenges to requirements that kept women out of particular jobs. But there also have been significant cases in which the challenge was to the employer's practice of assuming that the job could be done better by a woman.

Regardless of the nature of the challenge, however, the courts have tended to follow the same standard. That is, where the employer wants to argue that an individual's sex makes that individual better qualified, the employer has the burden of proving that there is a factual basis to believe that all, or substantially all, of the members of the opposite sex would be unable to perform the duties of the job safely and efficiently.

In a class action suit by males challenging an airline's policy of hiring only women as flight attendants, expert testimony was offered to prove that an airline cabin represents a unique environment that produces special psychological needs among the passengers and that these psychological needs are better attended to by females. In support of the policy, it was argued that the female attendants were superior to males in the aspects of the job that required providing reassurance to anxious passengers, giving courteous personalized service and, making flights as pleasurable as possible within the limitations imposed by aircraft operations.

The policy was found to be illegal, however, because it could not be shown that the essence of the business operation would be undermined by not limiting the position to women. The court went on to say that its ruling did not prevent the airline from taking "into consideration the ability of *individuals* to perform the non-mechanical functions of the job." But, the court emphasized, the airline "cannot exclude *all* males simply because *most* males may not perform adequately." [28]

Different courts have applied slightly different standards for determining whether a person's sex is a legitimate qualification (known technically as a BFOQ, or bona fide occupational qualification). In general, however, the intent of Congress and the regulations of the EEOC have been interpreted by the courts to mean that such a requirement can be a BFOQ only if it is an actual sexual characteristic rather than a characteristic that might, to one degree or another, correlate with a particular sex.[29] Such impermissible stereotypes include, for example, that men are less capable of assembling intricate equipment or that women are less capable of aggressive salesmanship.[30]

No doubt one reason for Mark's willingness to accept that certain characteristics may be attributed to women generally

---

[28]*Diaz v. Pan American World Airways,* 442 F.2d 385, 388 (5th Cir.), *cert. denied* 404 U.S. 950 (1971) (emphasis in original).

[29]*See Rosenfeld v. Southern Pacific Co.,* 444 F. 2d 1219 (9th Cir. 1971).

[30]*See* EEOC Guidelines on Sex Discrimination, 29 C.F.R. § 1604.2 (a), stating that the principle of nondiscrimination requires that individuals be considered on the basis of individual capacities and not on the basis of any characteristics generally attributed to the group.

is the belief that in this situation the generalization is being used to benefit a woman rather than to her detriment. In the employment context, however, courts have read our EEO laws as prohibiting judgments based upon stereotypes, even where the stereotype may be seen as a positive characteristic. For example, in the recent case alleging that an accounting firm's appraisal process was discriminatory, one judge noted that the degree to which the appraisals reflected stereotypes — positive or negative — indicated that the person being appraised was being looked at on the basis of her sex, which is contrary to the law.[31]

A company must take care to assure that discussions of cultural differences, promoted as part of a diversity initiative, do not themselves serve as a basis for continuing stereotypes. All too often, in an effort to point out a contrast in the styles of two individuals who are from different cultures, there is a tendency to speak of particular traits or characteristics as though they would be found in every single person from a particular country or part of the world.

Indeed, the willingness of apparently well-intentioned people to engage unknowingly in stereotyping is documented all too clearly when we look back at statements made in earlier days. For example, as society honors the achievements of Lech Walesa and Solidarity in Poland, it

---

[31]*Hopkins v. Price Waterhouse,* 825 F.2d 458 (D.D.C. 1987), *reversed in part,* 109 S.Ct. 1775 (1989). An interesting counterpoint to the situation in *Hopkins* can be seen in *Fadhl v. City and County of San Francisco,* 741 F.2d 1163, 1165 (1984). In that case, the plaintiff was criticized for behaving "too much like a woman" in her police officer training and she was advised not to look too much "like a lady" because that could cause problems in her work.

seems difficult to understand the actions of labor organizations at the turn of the century who refused to accept Polish workers as members because the unions believed that Polish workers did not have the capacity to be good union members. It is similarly difficult to believe that stereotypes about Italian-Americans were so commonly accepted in 1939 that *LIFE* magazine felt free to point out that baseball star Joe DiMaggio, who grew up in San Francisco, "speaks English without an accent and is otherwise well adapted to most U.S. mores," keeps his hair slick with water "instead of olive oil," and "never reeks of garlic. . . ."[32] There are, of course, many examples of such thinking about many of the cultures that make up our society.

What is surprising, however, is that today even some of the experts who are otherwise sensitive to diversity management issues nonetheless generalize about "cultural traits or characteristics" and are comfortable attributing such characteristics to each individual who happens to be a member of a particular group. Thus it has been suggested that whites and blacks have different styles of managing or that whites and blacks have different styles of arguing. For example, one consultant has suggested that whites, when arguing, tend to move toward each other and touch the other person's shoulder to calm him down and that blacks find this touching to be threatening. While this may be true for some whites, and for some blacks, it certainly is not true of everyone. The useful information — that one person's actions or style in an animated discussion or argument may be misinterpreted by another — is a valid part of an awareness session. To make this point, however, it is not

---

[32]Life Magazine, May 1, 1939, at 69.

necessary to convey the (inaccurate) impression that a particular trait is found in every member of a particular group. Other consultants have suggested that in one culture the family is considered more important than the individual while in another culture the reverse is true, or that self-sacrifice is considered important in one culture but is considered unhealthy in another. Such information can be useful in reminding us that different cultures may promote different values. But when such information is conveyed as being the standard for all Asians, or all whites, it carries the same flaws as any other racial or ethnic stereotype. Such generalizations have no place in the employment decisions made about individuals from either of these cultures.[33]

3. The Legal Restriction on Stereotypes

The challenge of dealing with individuals from a variety of racial and ethnic backgrounds brings us face-to-face with a subject that has long been at the heart of our principles of

---

[33]Typically, another topic raised during diversity planning sessions involves the relationship between the company's effort to promote awareness of diversity in the United States workforce and the company's efforts to compete in international markets and to manage the workforce at facilities located overseas. Obviously companies find there is a lot to be learned from the people working with their overseas operations. At the same time, it must be remembered that there are some very significant differences between preparing to confront Japanese culture *in that country* and preparing to manage a workforce that may include some Japanese Americans. Again, the goal is to be able to deal with employees as individuals, regardless of their background. Many people talk about the "Japanese way" of doing business or how the culture in Japan influences management style in that country. For purposes of employment decisions in this country, those kinds of cultural generalizations (or stereotypes) have no place in a manager's dealings with individual employees who may be of Japanese origin.

equal employment opportunity. That is, the process of assuring that our system of human resources management is marked by rational decision-making and avoids reliance on improper generalizations and stereotypes. From a legal perspective, one of the most often-cited discussions of stereotypes is found in the Supreme Court's decision in a case involving retirement plan contributions.[34]

The case involved a challenge to an employer's practice of requiring women employees to make larger contributions to the retirement plan than the men employees were required to make. The employer's justification for this practice was that women, as a class, live longer than men. The Court, noting that there are both real and fictional differences between men and women, pointed out that it is now well recognized that employment decisions cannot be based on an employer's stereotyped impressions about the characteristics of males or females. "Myths and purely habitual assumptions about a woman's inability to perform certain kinds of work are no longer acceptable reasons for refusing to employ qualified individuals, or for paying them less."[35]

The employer's decision in this case, however, involved a generalization that was unquestionably true — statistics demonstrate that women, as a class, do live longer than men. Thus, the employer argued, there was a factual basis for treating women employees and men employees differently. But, the Court was not persuaded. While it is true that, as a

---

[34]*City of Los Angeles, Department of Water v. Manhart,* 435 U.S. 702 (1978).

[35]*Id.* at 707.

class, women have been living longer than men, it is equally true that all the individuals in these two respective classes do not share this characteristic. That is, some women do not live as long as the average man, and some men outlive the average woman.

The Court went on to explain that the existence or nonexistence of discrimination is a question that focuses on the *individual.* The law prohibits an employer from treating any individual as simply a component of a racial, sexual, or ethnic class. Even a true generalization about a class is an insufficient reason for disqualifying an individual to whom the generalization might not apply.[36]

This aspect of the law presents several important cautions for the manager who tries to understand his or her employees by studying the culture of the racial or ethnic group to which those employees belong. For example, a manager who has several Asian employees may studiously read several of the current volumes about how the Japanese do business. Such study may be very positive in terms of

---

[36]As the courts have dealt with the issue of stereotypes, they have pointed out that such thinking can involve several different types of flaws. First, the notion may be entirely untrue. Second, the notion may be true about some people, or even true about many people in a group, but not true about everyone in a group. Admittedly, the legal approach to stereotypes in the workplace is more restrictive than the approach to stereotypes taken by some other professionals. But, the effective approaches to diversity management reflect the same distrust found in the court decisions. *See* L. Copeland, *Learning to Manage a Multicultural Workforce,* Training (May 1988) ("Some experts say stereotypes are not necessarily bad — it's what we do with them. I disagree. Stereotypes are bad because they are so powerfully effective in preventing differentiated thinking about people who belong to the stereotyped group.").

broadening one's cultural perspectives. But when faced with the prospect of managing Asian employees, the manager must be sharply aware of the limits of such knowledge.

First, the categories we use for creating an EEO-profile of our workforce are very rough categories. Within the Asian category are many different and varied cultures. Similarly, the term Hispanic includes many individuals who, while sharing a Latin or Spanish background, come from quite different cultures.[37]

Second, even if our manager has focused simply on learning about Japanese culture in order to deal better with Japanese employees, the manager must be aware that, even if the facts he learns are as firmly based in statistics as the conclusion that women outlive men, the manager should avoid basing any employment decisions on these cultural differences. There is no certainty that each individual shares these characteristics.[38]

Indeed, experts warn of the frustration experienced by individuals who, for one reason or another, do not fit the particular cultural mold associated with their background.

---

[37] See, for example, the discussion of the different social origins and cultural differences found among Mexicans, Puerto Ricans, Cubans, Dominicans, Central and South Americans, and descendants of the Spaniards who settled in the Southwestern United States, in *The Hispanic Population of the United States,* by F.D. Bean and M. Tienda (1987).

[38] In discussions of cultures, it must also be kept in mind that cultures — by their very nature — change slowly, but they do change. It cannot be assumed that in other cultures, any more than in one's own, cultural beliefs or traits are shared by everyone regardless of age, status, or other characteristics.

For example, imagine an individual of Japanese origin who has spent years — or even a lifetime — in a Western environment, but finds himself being treated as though he had spent his entire life in Japan.[39]

Thus, the wisdom of the Supreme Court's decision is that, even where it is possible to have a firm understanding of a difference between racial or ethnic groups, that difference cannot be the basis for employment decisions with respect to individuals that happen to belong to those groups.

With this in mind, it can be instructive to examine the apparent difference in the way two cultures deal with humor. Assuming there is an actual basis for the statement that people in Japan often fail to appreciate American humor, an American politician who often relies on humor in his speeches would probably be well-advised to be cautious in his use of humor in a presentation to a large delegation of business executives from Japan. On the other hand, an American manager who sometimes uses his sense of humor as an indirect way of communicating a point to an employee would not necessarily need to change this practice simply because an individual of Japanese origin has come to work for him. What the manager should do, and what he probably should have been doing all along with *all* employees, is to be sparing with the use of such an indirect technique for communication unless he is certain from his knowledge of the individual that the message is being clearly understood.[40]

---

[39]*See* M. F. Deutsch, *Doing Business with the Japanese* 79-80 (1983).

[40]For an example of the differences in style that can exist between two white males in the same business who share similar values, consider the following description by former Congressional Leader Tip O'Neill of his

Thus, as noted at the outset, managing a diverse workforce demands skills in the art of communicating with people, and understanding differences demands skill in the art of appreciating individual differences and similarities.

---

relationship with former President Jimmy Carter. "Although Carter and I came from vastly different backgrounds, we grew to appreciate each other. This took time, however, and required some adjustment on both sides," O'Neill explains. Noting that typically northern politics is much more blunt than southern politics, O'Neill observes that it took him a long time to understand President Carter's manner, or "to realize, for example, that his silence on a particular topic didn't necessarily mean acquiescence. . . . Jimmy Carter was so polite and gracious that he was often reluctant to express open disagreement. This took some getting used to, as I was accustomed to dealing with politicians who told you straight out when they thought you were wrong . . . . This minor lack of communication may sound insignificant, but these expressions are part of the chemistry that helps people work together effectively." T. O'Neill, *Man of the House* 364-365 (1987).

CHAPTER VI

EXAMINING THE CORPORATE CULTURE

Diversity management initiatives can differ significantly in both form and substance from one company to another. One key to producing a successful initiative has been to develop an approach that is adequately tailored to the needs and culture of a particular company. This requires a candid assessment of the employment practices and culture in the particular corporation or workplace. In some cases, this is the very first step in the initiative. In other instances, this assessment is an ongoing process, closely tied to the aspects of the initiative focused on improvement of communication and communication channels. Among the companies interviewed for this book, a variety of approaches were used to audit corporate cultures.

The assessment of workplace practices and the workplace culture can have several distinct objectives. One is to identify policies and procedures that have made the culture unnecessarily "exclusive" rather than "inclusive" and, if possible, to eliminate or modify them. By its very nature, this segment of the initiative will focus on changes in the existing culture and those who are part of it. A second objective is to reach out to those in the company who have been excluded from the culture to give them the knowledge and tools they need to become a successful part of the corporation and its culture.

Generally, the companies examined in the preparation of this paper found it practical to fashion initiatives that addressed both objectives. The primary considerations are reflected in the following conversation between **Mark** and **Lydia** as they try to map out a work plan for the diversity management task force.

Mark: I'm relatively new to all of this. I still have a lot to learn about our own "corporate culture," as we call it. But, from what I've seen, I assume corporate cultures tend to reflect the values of the people who have been running the corporation. And, let's be honest about it, most of those people are white males. How do we convince them that we need to make changes in the corporate culture? It's their culture, isn't it?

Lydia: Well, I can't say you're off base. Over the years, most of the people with most of the power have been white males. And, for the most part, they are the group we need to "sell" on the diversity initiative. But, of course, one of the things in life I have always found encouraging is that not all white males are alike. As proof, look at the corporations in this town. Each one of them is run by the same type of folks, but there are some real cultural differences from one company to another. I've seen some changes here that I know haven't happened at some of the other firms in town. Frankly, I think those differences have been the reason we have been so much more successful than the others at attracting and keeping females in management positions.

Mark: Okay. There is a strong competitive element here. In one sense, we simply need to change our corporate culture a little more or a little faster than the other corporations that compete with us for talent. That's a legitimate goal, even if it is somewhat modest.   But, in a bigger sense, how do you think we should approach the question of cultural changes?

Lydia: Well, from a legal point of view . . . .

Mark: This time, I don't want the legal point of view. I want your opinion as someone who has been part of this culture for some time.   Have you seen any changes in the culture since you started here?

Lydia: Oh yes!   For one thing, there's been a big improvement in the use of sports analogies.

Mark: What?

Lydia: When I first came to work here, the law department was almost all men.   After law school, though, I wasn't surprised by that.   What I wasn't prepared for, though, was how many of the guys used sports analogies to explain things. I was new, and I wanted to impress them that I was smart. But, I wasn't on the football team in college. I often had to ask for explanations. It became sort of a joke. But, over time, people got better about it.

Mark: That's ironic. Actually, I've found that sports is often one subject I can use to talk to guys with whom I might have very little in common. When one of the local teams is having a good year, anyone and everyone seems to get caught up in the spirit. And, you know, baseball is a big sport in Japan and in Latin America. That can cut through a lot of barriers.

Lydia: Good point.   Use whatever you can to overcome those barriers.   My point was simply that, in my case, the references to sports were not working as communication tools. Managers need to be sensitive to the fact that not everyone shares their background. When they see that a particular tool is not working to convey the intended message, they need to consider making a change. But, to get back to your question about whether we have the capacity to change, I assume you were thinking about something more significant than sports references.

Mark: Well, everyone has his or her own perspective.

Lydia: Okay, seriously, I've been here long enough to see a lot of change. I know we have the capacity to change as an organization. It's slow — at times painfully slow. But it does happen. I've also been here long enough to know that some things don't change very easily. I would like to think that we can have a workplace where differences are appreciated. And I'm confident we can make progress in that direction, but — knowing people as I do — I guess I'm not quite sure we're going to get all the way there, at least not for a long, long time. Meanwhile, there are people whose careers are developing, and happening right now. I think we'll run into some people who — because their career is moving along all right — are going to say let's not make any hasty changes. And, we're going to run into other people who feel the culture is not working in their favor and who will say that change needs to come quickly or it will be too late for their careers.

Mark: Okay. So, how does that translate in terms of our diversity initiative?

Lydia: I think it means we need to be prepared for criticism that we're going too fast as well as criticism that we're moving too slowly. The most effective response we will have

— in both situations — is to be able to point to our initiative as something that proceeds from a logical plan, driven by some rational and solid business judgments. To the extent that the initiative appears to be based on nothing more than our own sense of cultural rights and wrongs, we're going to be a fair target for emotional criticisms from all corners.

Mark: How do we define the goals for our project? I'd like to feel we are setting some targets that will make us stretch. You never know what you can accomplish until you try.

Lydia: Well, I guess what I'd like to see is. . . well, it's really several things. I would like to see us making a firm commitment to be headed in the right direction, and yet I want to see us do that without raising any false expectations or hopes that getting there will be easy or quick. At the same time, I want to see us committed to short term actions that maximize opportunities for the people here now. So, to answer your question, I want to see us make as much progress as we can. I just don't want to promise more than we can deliver. And I'm not certain changes in corporate culture — changes in the rules — can be delivered overnight. What we can deliver, almost overnight though, is a "guide" to the corporate culture to help people understand the rules.

Mark: That sounds good. But I'm not very comfortable with the idea of changing the individual, rather than changing the culture. For example, in your case, it would have meant expecting you to learn all about sports just so you could understand what people were talking about. That's not very practical.

Lydia: In my case, actually, what some men started doing was supplementing their sports analogies with other references I could understand. That way, they communicated their point and at the same time I gradually learned a few of the more important sports concepts. For example, I now understand what someone means when he says, "It's time to punt." So, I think it's fair to say that there was change on both sides. But you raise a very good point. What if the situation involved not simply a difference in backgrounds, but a difference tied to a critical element of a person's culture?

Mark: Yes. And, if the company indicated it expected the individual to change, couldn't that be construed as forcing the individual to "give up" something that may be an important part of that person's cultural heritage? How do we handle that? What does the law say?

Lydia: It depends upon what the change involves. You remember our talk about burdens of proof and the importance of consistency in employment policies?

Mark: Yes. . . yes.

Lydia: Well, some of those same considerations would apply. But essentially the law would give us a lot of leeway, and in many cases it would come down to our decision, from an employee relations standpoint, as to whether we believed we could accommodate the difference.

Mark: And, I assume one of the reasons for this whole exercise is we believe there may be areas where we can be — and maybe have to be — more accommodating if we are going to attract and keep the caliber of workers we need.

Lydia: How much we can or should expect people to change is an aspect that deserves careful attention. The program must be seen as an effort to make sure everyone has the opportunity to understand the rules, not an effort to drain the culture from individuals. And, ultimately the goal is to give individuals enough information to decide whether they wish to "buy in" to the corporate culture.

Mark: And, to the extent we as an employer make the "buy in" price too high, we are going to find ourselves having difficulty getting and keeping the people we need.

Lydia: That's the incentive for us as an employer to make sure that the price is no higher than it has to be.

Mark: But, before we can even know whether the price is too high, we have to know how the price is calculated. A manager who is insensitive may not even understand what the currency is for many of the employees.

Lydia: For example?

Mark: Well, there are a lot of people here who are dedicated to their jobs and the company, but who are also dedicated to their families. When we set policies, or follow practices, that force them to choose between the company and their family, we are exacting a price. We should recognize that. Of course, recognizing that will not always mean we can change the policy or the practice. Perhaps, there will be times when the company has to make demands and the employee has to make some hard choices. But, we should know about that. Otherwise we are likely to force those hard choices more times than we really need to, and we are likely to lose quality people who find our price unnecessarily high.

Commentary

For most companies that have made successful efforts in promoting diversity management, the initiative has involved at least two prongs. That is, one part of the initiative has been aimed at examining the corporate culture, including employment practices and policies, and modifying some aspects of that culture to promote inclusiveness. The second prong also begins with an examination of the corporate culture. But, its goal is somewhat different. When an examination of the corporate culture identifies a business policy or practice that, while entirely legitimate, appears to be acting as a barrier to individuals of a certain background, it may not always be possible or practical to change that policy. Rather, the practical approach may be to focus efforts on education and/or communication to eliminate or minimize the impact of that policy on those individuals.

1. Lessons from History

The importance of proceeding with both prongs of such an initiative is not without historical precedent. There have been periods in American history when issues somewhat similar to those being discussed today faced employers and union leaders as a result of significant numbers of new immigrants coming to this country and joining the workforce. In those situations, the more successful efforts to bring together immigrants and native workers in a "multi-cultural" workforce focused on the importance of communicating with individuals in both of these groups and stressing those areas where there was a common interest.[41]

---

[41] See W.M. Leiserson, *Adjusting Immigrant and Industry* 186-87, 236 (1924).

For example, one major steel producer recognized that the company's interest in production and safety could be served by undertaking efforts to improve the English language skills of immigrant workers. And, a major auto manufacturer initiated similar efforts to improve literacy among its workers.[42] On the other hand, history also records the statements of the president of a mining company who declared that there was no business purpose served by improving the literacy or language skills of the workers. [43] While there are many factors that contribute to a company's continued success over time, it is interesting to note that the auto manufacturer and the steel producer exist today as major American corporations. The mining company is no longer in business.

Efforts were directed at various groups of miners, however, by various union organizers. One of the successful efforts in the anthracite coal regions started by identifying two priorities: First, there was a need for education of the native workers to overcome prejudice toward the immigrants, dwelling "upon the importance of treating the newcomers as equals, and appeal[ing] to the native-born workers to discard derisive names like 'Hunky' and 'Dago' and if they could not pronounce the foreigners' surnames to address them by their Christian names." Second, there was a need to educate the

---

[42]H. Feldman and J. S. Ozer, *Racial Factors in American Industry,* 276-278 (1971).

[43]Leiserson, at 65.

foreign workers in the "importance of being business-like, and the necessity of building up a strong organization." [44]

Today, the ingredients of a successful program for managing diversity are likely to go well beyond those efforts of the 1920's, but the keys to success will continue to be the extent to which the employer is able to modify its existing culture to emphasize inclusion rather than exclusion and the extent to which employers are able to provide individuals from a variety of backgrounds with an environment that allows them to take full advantage of the opportunities offered by the company.

2. Approaches for Analyzing the Culture

For many companies the first step has been as simple as a presentation, or series of presentations, designed to convey information about the changing demographics, their impact on the workforce, and the need for greater awareness of these changes. Typically, an initial presentation is made to upper level executives in the course of deciding what actions will be included in the company's diversity initiative. In such a presentation, the *Workforce 2000* projections about the changing demographics of the labor force can be very compelling to anyone who has not heard them previously. It is generally more effective to supplement those numbers with company-specific data. The year 2000 may seem distant, but the workforce data for most companies already reflects the changing mix of workers.

---

[44]*See* Leiserson, at 186-187. *See also,* J. Barbash, *Ethnic Factors in the Development of the American Labor Movement,* Interpreting the Labor Movement 71-73 (1952).

The second step is to identify potential problems, and develop programs and initiatives to respond to them. In doing so, some companies have undertaken a process that amounts to a "cultural audit" of their workforce and employment practices.[45] The process may involve surveys of employees, or discussions with small groups of employees. It may also involve many of the same techniques of statistical analysis commonly used in doing EEO and affirmative action audits.

Two critical aspects of the corporate culture must be addressed. They are, first, assessing the "culture" of the company itself, and second, determining how the individuals coming into the company (or already there) can best be helped to understand — and to decide to accept — the culture of the company.

The assessment of corporate or workplace culture requires candid input from a variety of sources. It requires looking at company practices and traditions in some detail. One approach is to focus on the careers of individuals who have been successful within the company. What paths did their careers follow? What experiences are common to all or most of these individuals? Many times these individuals themselves can be a useful source of information, but they should not be the only source and need not be the only focus.

----

[45]One of the most refined approaches to cultural audits is that developed by Dr. Roosevelt Thomas of the American Institute for Managing Diversity described briefly in *From Affirmative Action To Affirming Diversity,* Harvard Business Review, March - April 1990, at 107, 114. A series of considerations sometimes used in "reading" a corporate culture are listed in T. E. Deal and A. A. Kennedy, *Corporate Cultures: The Rites and Rituals of Corporate Life* 129-139 (1982).

It may also be helpful to look at the careers of individuals who were not successful in meeting either the company's expectations or their own. What do their careers have in common, and what patterns can be seen when comparing them to the first group?

Finally, it can be useful to analyze the careers of those who appeared to be successful but who chose to leave the company rather than stay. What were their reasons? Today, as the post-World War II generation competes for fewer management opportunities, many talented individuals have chosen to leave large corporations to try their hand at running their own businesses. Is the desire to be an entrepreneur the sole reason, or did the person leave because of a belief that he or she had no future with the corporation?

3. The Dilemma of Unwritten Rules

Another useful approach is to assess candidly what are, or what are perceived to be, the so-called unwritten rules for success at the company. There may be unwritten rules that are at odds with the company's EEO responsibilities, such as an assumption that certain jobs are not really appropriate for a woman. Some of these rules may have a "factual" basis, such as "we had a woman in that job once and it didn't work out because she did not like the frequent travel." Obviously, such rules could not survive in written form. They would be both illegal and embarrassing. They must not be allowed to exist in unwritten form either.

There may also be more subtle restrictions based on the comfort level of certain people who say they "simply prefer to work with people whom they already know." One way to counteract this attitude is to make sure that person has numerous opportunities to get to know a broader variety of people.

Finally, some unwritten rules are not in and of themselves discriminatory, but rather based on some traditional value or values of the company. Such values may relate to a particular style of management or any of a number of other very significant issues. They may also relate to matters of lesser significance, such as dress styles. In either instance, a similar form of analysis is called for, as illustrated in the following discussion among **Mark, Lydia,** and **Gene.**

Mark: Here's one example I'd like your opinion on. While I was in business school, I had a job working at one of those "old line" financial firms in New York. The company's reputation is closely tied to its image as a very safe place for people to do business. Well, even though no one told me, it didn't take me long to realize that they had a dress code.

Lydia: You mean something like, "Everyone who comes into contact with customers must wear a blazer?"

Mark: Sort of, but actually blazers were acceptable only for those of us at the very bottom. I heard that anyone who hoped to get promoted — to vice president, for example — had to dress in a way that reflected the firm's conservative business image. No blazers; no light suits; no bright ties; and no polyester. It was an unwritten rule: If you don't wear the appropriate dark suits, you won't get promoted to the upper ranks.

Gene: Was that really a rule?

Mark: Several people told me about it.

Gene: What I mean is, from our perspective, the first question to decide is whether the so-called "unwritten rule" is actually a rule. That is, when people at the firm are being considered for promotion, is their style of dress actually a factor?

Mark: For purposes of discussion, let's assume it is. What then?

Gene: Then the question is, should this rule be changed?

Lydia: Legally, I think the firm could argue that a dress code is related to its business. So long as the code doesn't discriminate, it shouldn't pose a legal problem.

Gene: So, the question remains simply, does management want to use style of dress as a criterion for selecting executives? If they decide that they do, then they should acknowledge that this is a factor.

Mark: I guess I still question whether the style of a person's clothing indicates anything about his financial skills.

Gene: A legitimate question, perhaps. But, that's one that — for purposes of our exercise — we let the executive office decide. If they are wrong, or unnecessarily restrictive, they may find themselves having a difficult time recruiting and keeping the people they need. For purposes of improving our ability to manage a diverse workforce, it's the next decision that is more important. Once it's decided that style of dress *is* a factor, how can we make sure that standard is communicated to everyone?

Lydia: So you are less concerned with the "rule" than with the "unwritten" nature of it.

Gene: Absolutely. One of the most frequent casualties in a diverse workforce is communication. And, one of the things that most often is not communicated is the "unwritten rule." Too often, it's going to be the person who is different — the black or Hispanic, for example, in a predominantly white workforce — who never hears about the unwritten rules.

Mark: Well, what if it's not an absolute rule? Perhaps there was one fellow with a polyester suit who become a vice president five years ago.

Lydia: Legally we'd have a tough time defending a *written* rule that was applied sometimes and not others. The standard is no different simply because it's unwritten. If generally the way a person dresses is something that is not overlooked in the promotion process, then it is enough of a "rule" or "policy" that we should scrutinize it.

Gene: The assessment process would go something like this: Do we need this policy? Is there some legitimate job-related reason for this? This question may be answered yes or no. The critical answer is the response to the *next* question. If we do not need the rule, then how do we go about getting rid of it? Specifically, how do we go about letting decision-makers know that the unwritten dress code is not to be a factor in eliminating people from jobs?

On the other hand, if we decide that this dress code is a good policy — say because our image as a traditional, conservative business is important to us, and we feel that how our executives dress is a reflection of that image — then how do we communicate that to all employees?

Lydia: So, the influx of people from diverse cultures doesn't mean we have to throw out all of the customs and cultures we have developed. It does mean that we have to make efforts to assure that the customs we do have are communicated in an orderly way to all employees.

Gene: That's right. If we follow our traditional approach of letting things like this be filtered down through the grapevine, we take the risk that those employees who are different may just never get the word.

Lydia: Okay, I have an example for you. One of our human resources managers in California told me about a situation there last year. One of our employees — a very good employee — left, and he told the exit interviewer that he was leaving because he never had been considered for a promotion. That got the interviewer's attention because several months earlier another departing employee had made the same statement. And, an additional item of concern was that both individuals who left were of Asian background.

Mark: What was the procedure for promotions?

Lydia: When we looked into it, we found that the manager was quite candid in telling us his approach was that he would consider promoting anyone who came into his office and told him they wished to be considered. He remembered both employees. He said that they were both good workers but that he never had any indication from them that they wanted to be moved up. And when we checked the records, there was no indication of a discrimination problem. The manager had an excellent record on EEO and affirmative action.

Mark: Shouldn't he be taking a more direct interest in the careers of the people who work in his department?

Lydia: Ideally, yes. But, he says there is no time. He points out that his department has had all it could handle, meeting a series of big contract deadlines last year and more of the same this year. He says that when it comes to personnel matters, it's all he can do to keep on top of the people who are *not* doing their jobs.

Gene: That's not an uncommon complaint from managers. And, the recent reductions-in-force have often produced situations where managers now have responsibility for more people.

Lydia: That's exactly what he says. So, to him, it seems entirely logical to assume that anyone who wants a promotion or a transfer should come in and tell him so. Maybe some of that comes from his background — he is one of a number of managers at that facility who joined us after a career as a military officer. Maybe it's a practical outcome of the load we are putting on our managers.

Mark: On the other hand, we have to understand that in certain cultures, coming forward to ask for a promotion is simply not done. We can't keep losing good people simply because they interpret inattention from the manager as an indication that their career is at a dead-end.

Lydia: So, what do we do? Do we try to force the managers to change?

Gene: I think that should happen. But, in practical terms I don't know how far we can get. Maybe we need to focus some effort on helping people from different backgrounds understand the system. You know, make them more comfortable with the idea of going in to ask for a promotion.

Lydia: That's what I would recommend.

Mark: Yes. Hope for the best, but plan for the worst! So, how would we identify those individuals who need to be re-assured that going in to talk with the boss is okay?

Lydia: That's one of the best features of this re-examination of our culture. When we find problems or weak spots, we fix them for *all* of the employees. Granted, the problem came to our attention because two employees — both from an Asian background — left their jobs. But, once we examine the problem, we find it is a basic problem of communication.

Mark: Communicating the rules that are used to manage that workplace.

Lydia: Right. And, we solve the communication problem by making sure that the manager who wants to operate in this way, or who is operating in this way because of workload and other factors, at least takes the time to convey the rules to everyone.

Commentary

The discussion above highlights how the analysis of a culture's unwritten rules — even unwritten rules about relatively simple aspects of corporate life — can generate serious policy questions.   Throughout that discussion, it was assumed that the basic choices about what policy to follow were choices from among alternatives that are each entirely legal.   This will frequently be the case in an examination of the rules in a workplace that has a well-developed program of equal employment opportunity and affirmative action. Such programs, if pursued seriously, tend to force examination of the standards used in a workplace and the impact that such standards have.   Even where the unwritten rule does not have an illegal impact, however, the examination is an important process.

1.   Choosing Policies That Promote Inclusiveness

Whenever an examination of workplace culture uncovers a practice, or a series of practices, that has a significant adverse impact on a class of individuals protected by the civil rights laws, there are serious questions to be addressed by the employer.   Can the practice be justified on the basis of legitimate business reasons?   Is there some alternative that would serve the same business purposes without the same degree of negative impact?

Where the examination of an unwritten policy does not raise a legal issue of discrimination, of course, the employer has the option of simply maintaining the policy in the same manner it has been operating.   But, that option does not necessarily serve the interests of the diversity initiative.   Thus, the employer needs to try to clearly identify what business purpose is served by this unwritten policy.   If there is none, then it is easy enough to decide to eliminate the policy.   As noted in the discussion above, however, eliminating a policy that was never formally implemented or communicated can sometimes be more difficult than repealing or changing a policy that was issued in writing.

Frequently, the employer will find that the unwritten rule or policy serves some legitimate purpose. In that case, it is appropriate to explore how this rule or policy could be put in writing or at least systematically communicated (through a structured mentoring program or through a career development program, for example). At the same time, however, it is reasonable to examine the rule or policy to determine if there might be other ways to accomplish the same business purpose with an approach that seeks to include more people or to exclude fewer people. Is that policy, albeit a legitimate one, creating limitations that make it difficult for some individuals to use their talents and achieve their full potential in the workplace? It is the employers who are the most creative in responding to this inquiry that will have the most success in attracting and retaining the workers with needed skills.

In weighing the need for various policies and rules, remember that the problem with unwritten rules is not simply that some persons may never hear about the rule. Unwritten rules, by their nature, are subject to inconsistent interpretation and application. And management often suffers because even employees who learn about unwritten rules may never fully understand the reasons behind the rule. When communicating a policy or rule in a formal manner, management has the opportunity to clearly explain the policy, the rationale and reasons behind the policy, and how the policy is to be interpreted and applied. This makes it much easier for employees to "get on board" and adopt the values expressed in the policy as their own.

Indeed, where the employer does decide that a policy or a standard must remain intact because it appears to be the very best way to serve important business purposes, the employer may want to consider whether there are efforts it can make — beyond simply communicating the policy — to assist employees in complying with that policy or in meeting that standard.[46]

The task of examining a corporate culture is of course a complex undertaking. The contrasting concerns that are called into consideration during such a process are not unlike the concerns expressed by educators as they have debated the curriculums in our schools. To what extent is there a core of knowledge which must be universal in order to assist us in working together and communicating with one another? To what extent must this universal core be ever-changing to reflect the ever-changing nature of our society and to assure the inclusion of all elements of our society?

---

[46]To eliminate the barriers to individual success within an organization, it is important to identify which barriers the organization can eliminate and which barriers the individual can affect. In a report identifying the barriers blocking the progress of minorities into management positions, the Upward Mobility Committee of the Program to Increase Minorities in Business (PIMIB) has suggested that the balance between these two types of barriers is such that "the individual has the responsibility for addressing and evaluating his or her role" within the organization, and the employer has responsibility for creating an environment where "corporate culture, values, and goals work together" to facilitate upward mobility. *Minorities in Management,* prepared by the PIMIB Task Force of the American Assembly of Collegiate Schools of Business, at 8. As an employer examines its culture and practices, of course, it may discover that there are ways it can provide assistance to those individuals seeking to overcome individual barriers.

An easily understood example of the interplay among these competing considerations is seen in one educator's recent description of how his father had often included allusions to Shakespeare as a way of making a point in business letters.[47] In this manner, a simple phrase from one of Shakespeare's works could be used to convey a meaning that might otherwise take a number of sentences or even paragraphs. On the other hand, this manner of communication presumed that the reader of the letter had a background in Shakespeare's writings and would understand, immediately and precisely, the meaning of the reference.

Such a practice — that is, communicating key business points by using allusions to Shakespeare — provides a simple example of how certain practices that once may have been quite effective now may have an exclusionary effect and need to be re-examined and modified. The examination process would proceed as follows: Can it be assumed that the audience for such communications shares a common literary background that includes Shakespeare?[48] If not, are we

---

[47]*See* E.D. Hirsch, Jr., *Cultural Literacy: What Every American Needs to Know* 9 (1987).

[48]Hirsch concludes, "The moral of this tale is not that reading Shakespeare will help one rise in the business world. My point is a broader one. The fact that middle-level executives no longer share literate background knowledge is a chief cause of their inability to communicate effectively." *Id.* at 9-10.

The Hirsch treatise on cultural literacy demonstrates the difficult task that is involved in trying to define a "culture." In his book, Hirsch and several colleagues attempted to illustrate American literary culture by compiling a list of the terms (such as names of famous people, historical events, geographic names, etc.) that make up the range of knowledge shared by Americans. When first published, the "preliminary list"

willing to live with the fact that a segment of our audience is not likely to understand whatever message is being communicated? To the extent that we are not prepared to simply write off a segment of our audience, or to the extent that we hope to *broaden* our intended audience, we need to overcome the problems created by this style of communication.

If such a communication problem exists in the workplace and the manager fails to make modifications, the manager creates a dilemma for employees. A practical employee who — for example — has skills the employer needs but whose background does not include a knowledge of Shakespeare is forced to make a choice. Such an employee would need to consider either learning something of this literature to be able to succeed in the prevailing culture of the workplace, or finding a business environment where such a background is not a prerequisite. In a labor market where there is a shortage of skilled workers, the second choice often will be both appealing and available.

Of course, in this particular example, once our Shakespearean manager understands the need to change his communication style, actually making the change should not be too difficult. This is not always the case in other situations. Making a change in management style, or

---

contained 4,500 items. *Id.* at 152-215. Shortly after this list was published, however, other authors put together supplementary lists indicating that the Hirsch list had not included all aspects of the culture. See, for example, R. Simonson and S. Walker, *Multi-Cultural Literacy* at 191-200 (Graywolf Annual 5, 1988). The lesson for the employment setting is that when attempting to define or analyze the corporate culture, efforts must be made to examine issues from a broad perspective.

changing the corporate culture, can be a formidable task. The slowness with which cultural change occurs, however, is itself a phenomenon that tends to promote communication and understanding — among those who are already a part of that culture. This natural resistance to overnight change serves to underscore the need for the two-pronged approach discussed above. That is, to the extent that a desired change in the culture may take time, it is imperative to also undertake efforts to "educate" those who are faced with the immediate challenge of operating within the existing culture.

The experience of the employers interviewed for this book confirmed the fact that cultural change *can* be accomplished, but seldom do those accomplishments occur quickly or easily. Thus, the willingness of an employer generally, and of individual managers, specifically, to engage in efforts to "educate" people about the current corporate culture are often critical to the success of diversity initiatives. Indeed, at times the succes of "educational" efforts to create a universal understanding of what the corporate culture is can be more important than the specific choices about what the corporate culture should be.[49]

---

[49]Hirsch notes that it is a form of cultural chauvinism and provincialism to believe that the content of a particular vocabulary, or in our case, corporate culture, makes it inherently superior to others. "Think how well the French or Chinese have done without Shakespeare . . . ." The benefit of broadening our horizons by encountering other cultures, suggests Hirsch, is that we "discover not only that other cultures have produced other successful vocabularies for dealing with life, but also that all of the great national vocabularies, including our own, have a relativity about them . . . . The specific contents of the different national vocabularies are far less important than the fact of their being shared." *Id.* at 107.

CHAPTER VII

CHANGING THE CORPORATE CULTURE:
LEGAL REQUIREMENTS

In the previous chapter, the discussion about corporate culture emphasized that on many matters of corporate culture, the company has a choice of deciding what type of culture it wants to promote. The demographic and labor market changes discussed earlier mean that it will often be in the employer's interest to promote a culture that is more "inclusive" than "exclusive." Indeed, there are many positive characteristics and strengths to be drawn from a culture marked by diversity or pluralism. At the same time, however, this does not mean a company must forsake the values that it deems important. It is not necessary to allow the workplace culture to be so open or inclusive that it appears to be undiscerning.

One of the primary challenges to a pluralistic organization is that it must be something more than the sum of its parts. It is not sufficient to say simply that an organization respects the values of everyone and anyone. The organization must bring diverse individuals together while at the same time maintaining enough structure to impose across the organization those values that are fundamental to the organization itself. To put this into another context, there are values that the law *requires* the employer to include in its culture, regardless of whether those values are consistent with the values of each of the various elements of the pluralistic culture.

The best examples of such elements of the workplace culture are seen in those things that the law mandates, such as the prohibition on sex discrimination and sexual harassment. An employer is expected to take steps to provide employees with an environment that is free of harassment. Of course, cultures around the world differ significantly in their views of the relative roles of men and women. Some cultures might tolerate or even encourage attitudes toward women that would be considered demeaning or offensive here. But the law is quite clear that an employer in this country cannot tolerate an employee who manifests such attitudes in the workplace, even though the source may be a difference in cultural background. Thus the law makes it clear there are some differences that are not valued.[50] This point is examined by **Mark** and **Lydia** in the following dialogue.

Mark: As we have gone through our discussions of diversity, I can't help but notice that on point after point, you mention

---

[50]Of course, in a pluralistic world, we cannot assume that there is universal agreement about the value of diversity. There have been, and there continue to be, cultures in other parts of the world where homogeneity is looked upon as a significant strength. In our own country, however, where the diverse nature of our population is already well established, there appears to be no practical purpose, or legal basis, for focusing on this question. Instead, our emphasis must be on the issue of how best to manage that diversity. As one legal scholar has noted, "[T]he cultural base for American identity always depended on some sharing of values, some shared vision of what we are as a nation. The *Brown* decision [holding that segregated schools are unconstitutional] recognized that the only vision of America capable of being shared by us all is a vision in which all of us belong." K. L. Karst *Belonging to America* 183-184 (1989).

that the law provides some limitations on what we can do. I hope you realize that's so frustrating to us non-lawyers.

Lydia: It can be frustrating for lawyers, too. But, I hope you don't lose sight of the big picture. I think what we are attempting to do with our diversity management project is very much in line with the general spirit of the law. It's just that there are some cautions, some limits that we need to be aware of.

Mark: But see, that just makes me all the more impatient with "the Law." What we're trying to do here is a very positive undertaking, and I think the law should be encouraging us.

Lydia: Actually, there are several aspects to the law that seem to be pushing us in the direction of maintaining a more inclusive workplace, and a workplace that is more tolerant of individual differences. Indeed, in some ways the law is demanding that employers manage diversity and do it well.

Mark: For example?

Lydia: Well, the law about harassment is one area where it is very clear. Age harassment. Racial harassment. Sexual harassment. And, we are expected to set a standard that many people might find to be stricter than the standards society may tolerate outside of the workplace. For example, there is conduct that may be acceptable among customers in some clubs or restaurants, and there is off-color humor that may be acceptable at certain parties. But, that doesn't excuse us from maintaining a workplace free of harassment. The employment laws have set a higher standard. We can't get away with saying, "Well, that kind of thing happens when men and women get together."

Mark: What about a manager who jokes about a person because of his age? Poking fun at older people is a standard form of humor on television comedies.

Lydia: But, in the workplace, those kind of disparaging remarks would probably be age harassment. You see, originally, the EEO laws were considered a tool for opening doors, giving people an equal opportunity to get into the workplace. Harassment wasn't a significant EEO issue until we began to have a mix of people in the workplace. But, once a more diverse workplace became a reality, then the EEO laws became more concerned with how people are treated while they are at work.

Mark: So the law against harassment is relatively new?

Lydia: Actually, the laws are the same laws we've been talking about all along. But, the courts and agencies are now interpreting those same laws in a manner that treats harassment as a form of discrimination. When you think about it, it's logical to assume that as an employer makes efforts to attract and bring together a diverse workforce, it will also want — at a minimum — to take steps to prevent those individuals from being harassed because of their differences.

Mark: So, if a man in our workplace treats a woman employee in an offensive manner, that becomes the employer's business even though the employer normally takes great pains not to get involved in employees' personal lives.

Lydia: Absolutely.

Mark: Help me out here. We want to become more open, more accepting of the differences among people, more tolerant of some of those characteristics or traits that might be different. The company should focus strictly on whether or not a person does the job. Right? At the same time, though, when we talk about sexual harassment, for example, the company is supposed to prohibit certain types of conduct regardless of whether it impedes the person's ability to do the job. For example if an employee has a calendar in his work area that might be offensive to someone, we tell him he has to take the calendar down — even though the presence of the calendar doesn't affect his ability to do the job. At what point does the accommodation of individual differences become prohibition of other individual characteristics?

Lydia: Okay, let's take a real life example. We have a gentleman in the shipping department who is from an Eastern European country. He has taken a liking to one of the women who works in the customer service office. There has been no touching, no crude remarks. But, he has taken to writing her love letters, long flowery love letters, describing his strong feelings for her. She complained to us. We asked him about it; he acknowledged that the letters were his. When we told him that he should stop, he said that this was personal, and none of the company's business. We said we thought it was our business, because several of the letters had been delivered through company mail and because it was now affecting her job.

Mark: Is writing a love letter to someone sexual harassment?

Lydia: One? No. But, twelve? Especially where she has done nothing to encourage the letters and has asked him to stop? I think she could argue that that's going too far.

Mark: Excuse me, but why didn't the guy give up when she told him she wasn't interested?

Lydia: Well, that's the interesting point. We asked him that very question, and that's where cultural differences come into the picture. He says that this is the way a man approaches a woman in his country. Rather than confront her directly, especially when he does not know her very well, he writes her letters, telling her of his feelings. He says it is not unknown for a woman to first respond by indicating she is not particularly interested as a way to spur him to greater efforts. Then, he adds, again, that he doesn't see why this is the company's business. In his country, the matter is between the man and the woman.

Mark: So, what did we do?

Lydia: Well, he's not in his country any more. It's the company's business because the law says we are responsible for maintaining a workplace that's free of sexual harassment. So maybe there are some aspects to diversity that we do not value. The bottom line is that, on some questions, there is going to be a right and a wrong. And, on some questions, the company is allowed to draw a line and say this type of conduct is unacceptable in our workplace, regardless of what a person's background may be.

Mark: I understand. But, there is more. If we decide that there is some conduct that is acceptable and some conduct that is unacceptable, we need to make that clear. When the workplace was more mono-cultural, we could more readily assume that over time people would learn what the company found to be okay, and what was frowned upon. Now it is incumbent upon us to be more direct, more specific. To spell it out, so that it can be understood by everyone.

Commentary

A careful review of the development of the laws of equal employment opportunity would confirm Lydia's statements. The idea that the prohibition on sex discrimination includes a prohibition on sexual harassment was first addressed in regulations in 1980, and was confirmed by the Supreme Court in 1986. By that time many employers had already undertaken strong programs to educate their employees on this issue.

More recently, the EEOC has issued guidelines indicating that the law prohibiting age discrimination also prohibits harassment of individuals because of their age. [51] Thus, a supervisor's characterization of an older worker as "unable to learn new tasks," or permitting other workers to tell jokes about the older worker's age, can be — in and of itself — a violation of the law against age discrimination.

It is clear that, with or without legal prohibitions on harassment, an employer relying upon the contributions of a diverse group of individuals must strive to maintain a workplace that is respectful of individual differences. The particular challenge posed by the laws is that they emphasize

---

[51]EEOC Compliance Manual (BNA) 615:0024 (June, 1987).

the fact that in maintaining such a workplace, the employer is seeking to maintain a standard of conduct which is higher than that sometimes imposed or permitted by our society generally. Thus, an employer cannot reasonably expect that such a higher standard of conduct — respecting individual differences — can be maintained effectively without a continuing program of employee education, stressing the company's commitment to a harassment-free workplace.

In this context, it is worth observing that the law places some limitations on the extent to which an employer can tolerate "diversity" among its employees. There are some differences which are so far from the standards our society accepts that they cannot be tolerated. In addition, even some of the variations of behavior that society "tolerates" are outside the scope of what an employer can permit in its workplace. For example, there are "cultures" in our world that include as a fundamental part of their beliefs a refusal to accept people of certain other "cultures." Or, there are people who suggest that it is against their beliefs to work with someone of a different sex. These differences the law does not expect an employer to respect or accommodate.

The law does expect employers, and individual managers, to promote and maintain a workplace environment that is free of harassment, because ultimately such harassment undercuts the policy of equal employment opportunity.

CHAPTER VIII

SUPPORT GROUPS

The following week, as **Lydia** is exploring the scope of the company's diversity initiative, she and **Gene** find themselves discussing the role of employee support groups.

Lydia: In talking to other companies about diversity management issues, one of the approaches you hear mentioned a lot is the development of various employee support groups. I know we already have some groups like that at Megatech.

Gene: Yes, the black employees' group has been around for nearly ten years.

Lydia: I hear about it from time-to-time. Generally, how active has it been?

Gene: Well, as with any other organization, that depends on the membership of the group at any particular time. Sometimes our focus has been on the company's affirmative action efforts — for example, letting the company know that we are watching its progress. Other times, we have been more focused on providing information and intelligence to one another for career development purposes. And, each year, we sponsor a social event that raises money for a local charity. Actually, we have been very successful with the charity fundraising, and that has done a lot to establish us as a "legitimate" community organization. It makes us something more than simply a single-interest or self-interest group.

Lydia: I know that the company requires that such organizations not have exclusive membership policies. Do the members feel it should be limited to blacks?

Gene: That's something that has been debated quite a bit. There are some members who feel that a basic purpose of the organization is to allow black employees to relate to one another, and that the presence of white employees will diminish that interaction — put a chill on it. But, on the other hand, there are some of us who feel that the basic purpose of the group is to provide support for black employees so we can do a better job, and improve our position within the company.

We want to make the company more sensitive and responsive to some of our needs and interests, and we think that a restrictive membership policy — on balance — sends a negative message that undermines that purpose.

Having said all that, I should add that — while it's been discussed within our group — it has been strictly an academic question. Over the years there have been only a handful of non-blacks who have inquired about attending the meetings.

Lydia: Have the other employee support groups been as successful?

Gene: Most of them are of a much more recent vintage. Some are doing well, I hear. They have regular meetings and events, with good interest and attendance. Some others have had a problem maintaining the interest of their target group.

Lydia: I guess we can assume that where the interest in the support group is continuing, the group is serving its purpose.

Gene: Yes, but sometimes individuals within the support group come to expect too much of it. In fact, there are people outside the support group who make that same mistake. You see, as blacks, we have to be able to interact successfully with people in the company who are non-black. We can't limit ourselves, and expect to be successful in a company that is predominantly white. We stand to lose the most by limiting our relationships to people in our own group. And that's where the company needs to be making an effort. The black employees' support group is a good idea, it has been successful in serving its particular purpose. But, the company needs to be making initiatives and promoting an atmosphere in which people can interact smoothly with individuals who are not part of their group. I guess that's why I see the diversity management project as being so important.

Commentary

Employee support groups and similar organizations have been effective initiatives in some companies. The most successful support group programs seem to be ones that are designed as a resource to promote employee development and common interests. There are legal concerns a company needs to consider, however, in deciding whether to pursue such an initiative. Most successful groups are not accorded any special recognition as a means for management to communicate with employees. In other words, a black or white employee who is not a member of a support group has exactly the same status as an employee who is a member.

It is important to be realistic about knowing how much a support group initiative can accomplish. A candid assessment of the atmosphere in the workplace may be useful. If, for example, the workforce is one in which the employer can foresee conflict among employee factions or between employees and management if certain employees were to form a group identifying themselves as being of a certain race, religion, etc., it may be best to defer such an initiative until more sensitivity or awareness can be developed.

Legal Considerations

Before an employer decides to initiate or cooperate in the formation of such an employee group, it should take care to have its attorneys examine the potential legal implications of the company's actions. There are some problems that can be avoided. One example of such problems is reflected in a case that involved a committee formed by black employees of a company in Philadelphia.[52]

The purpose of the committee was to eliminate workplace practices that were seen by the employees as discriminatory. While company officials met with representatives of the committee on a number of occasions to discuss issues of general concern to black employees, the company refused to allow its meetings with the committee to become an avenue for discussing grievances of individual employees. In this regard, the company's treatment of the Black Grievance Committee differed from its treatment of another employee organization known as the Independent

---

[52]*Black Grievance Committee v. National Labor Relations Board,* 749 F.2d 1072 (3d Cir. 1984).

Group Association (IGA). The company did allow representatives of the IGA to present individual grievances on behalf of its members at monthly meetings with company officials. Neither of the two groups had ever been certified or formally recognized as the bargaining agent of the company's employees. In response to a claim of unfair labor practices filed by the Black Grievance Committee, a federal court of appeals ruled that the company did not have the legal right to accord one employee group privileged status over another group, where neither group represented a majority of the employees nor was seeking the status of exclusive bargaining agent.

The court's ruling in this case suggests that employers must be scrupulously even-handed in their dealings with groups representing different minority factions within the workplace. Privileges, benefits and perquisites granted to any one such organization should, whenever practical, be granted to all similar organizations on an equal basis.

A related problem arises where there is an incumbent union that represents a majority of the workers, but separate support groups seek to speak for particular employees within the workforce. In this situation, the support groups will sometimes have to subordinate their activities to the program of the incumbent union. A women's support group cannot, for example, seek to force the employer to deal with it on issues affecting rights of women employees, while the employer continues to deal with the regular union on issues related to hourly wage rates. This is because the National Labor Relations Act (NLRA), embodies the principal of "exclusive representation," which means that a union recognized as the representative of a *majority* of the employees in a given unit must be recognized as the *sole* representative of *all* the employees in that unit, whether or not they are members of that union. The employer is then forbidden to deal with any other organization purporting to represent all or any of those same employees.

Finally, another related problem employers should be aware of in dealing with employee support groups is that even in the absence of a recognized labor union, active management support for, or involvement in, the formation or operation of employee support groups may result in unfair labor practice charges under the NLRA. The NLRA prohibits employers from dominating or interfering with the formation or administration of any "labor organization," a term which it defines broadly enough to cover any employee group that exists, in whole or in part, to deal with the employer over job-related matters. This does not mean that an employer should not allow such groups to exist. On the contrary, to prohibit their existence would likely be seen as an infringement of employees' basic rights under the NLRA. Nor does it mean that an employer cannot make its facilities available to employee support groups for purposes of holding meetings and publicizing their activities. Rather, it means that employers should be wary of making substantial monetary contributions to such organizations, openly campaigning in support of their activities, or becoming heavily involved in their administration.

These potential problems in dealing with employee support groups can be avoided in most cases by taking an approach whereby the employer allows — even welcomes — the formation of such groups as forums in which employees can meet to exchange information and ideas with one another, but not as organizations that exist to represent any employees in dealings with management.

Initiation of such support groups is one area where the companies interviewed for this book reflected a broad variety of approaches and experiences. Some had many years of experience with such groups, others had seen such groups begin and then wither away. And, at least a few have resisted the concept, while trying to promote other opportunities for employees to network and to gain career development advice. Finally, a few companies that have promoted such support groups are now actively exploring options that will encourage more discussion and interaction across group lines. As with other aspects of a diversity initiative, efforts in this area tend to be more successful when they are tailored to the needs and culture of the particular company or workplace.

CHAPTER IX

ACCOMMODATING CULTURAL DIFFERENCES — AND TAKING ADVANTAGE OF THEM

In this chapter, the focus is on several specific examples that serve to demonstrate how companies have responded to issues, using both the principles of equal opportunity and the concept of respecting and accommodating individual differences.

Women in Non-Traditional Jobs

Part of the diversity in the workplace these days is certainly the diversity provided by the increasing numbers of women. But, there are still many jobs where it is unusual to see more than a few women.[53] When a woman does express an interest in a non-traditional jobs, companies such as those

---

[53]One recent study examined the sex composition of 335 occupations and found that in 154 of the occupations, 75 percent or more of the incumbents were male; and in 57 of the occupations, 75 percent or more of the incumbents were female. Trends indicate changes in the participation of women in jobs other than in the predominantly-female occupations. The greatest improvement in the distribution of working women in non-traditional work during the past decade was in management positions. The integration into craft occupations, however, has been slow. *See,* D. M. Fignart and B. R. Bergman, *Facilitating Women's Occupational Integration,* Background Monograph No. 26 for *Investing in People,* a report by the U.S. Department of Labor Commission on Workforce Quality and Labor Market Efficiency (1989).

interviewed for this project typically make a special effort to try to help her succeed in it. The following program demonstrates how easily we can accept things as fundamental, and just assume there can be no change. Yet, sometimes a modest change can make a big difference.

A particular company had undertaken a commitment to increase the number of women in its auto repair positions. The first step, of course, was to make sure that women who did apply were not rejected because of their sex; that is basic non-discrimination. However, not many women were applying for those positions, so outreach efforts were necessary; that is affirmative action in its purest form.

Even after all of this, however, as women were recruited and hired for the job, the company noticed that women were dropping out at a higher rate than men. It would have been easy at this point to assume that the female mechanics simply did not have the aptitude or the interest to stay with the job, since they were being treated the same way the company had been treating male mechanics for years. In other words, the company could easily have said, "We've done all we can. We gave them the same opportunity we gave the men, and it just didn't work. They failed to make the grade."

When the company studied the situation further, through in-depth interviews and research, it recognized that the women who had been responding to the company's recruitment effort were genuinely interested in this job opportunity. The problem was they did not come to the job with the same sort of background as most of the men the company hired. The women had not spent hours and hours under the hood of a car while they were growing up. This made for a significant difference in the experience levels of these new recruits when compared to the individuals who typically applied for and were hired as mechanics. The company's solution was to develop a more basic introductory training course, geared for people — male or female — who did not have the background of an auto enthusiast. With the revised training program, the dropout rate for the new recruits was reduced.

This example points out that, while some problems arise because employers fail to recognize the similarities between men and women, other problems arise because the employer fails to adequately recognize the differences among individuals. What the employer did there was to recognize a certain difference in experience levels and compensate for that difference, without doing anything contrary to the fundamental principles of equal employment opportunity.

The difficult part of the solution in the mechanics example was being willing to re-examine one of the "givens" in that situation. It is usually easier to assume that the problem is with the people who drop out, not with the company's training program.

Accommodating Cultural Differences

The next two examples involve situations that arose at more than one or two of the employers interviewed for this book. The first problem came to the attention of management at one company when several women complained to management that there was a waiting line in the rest room after lunch. They said one of the stalls was being tied up by a woman who was down on the floor, apparently mumbling to herself. Investigation revealed that it was one of the newer employees whose religion required her to kneel down and pray several times a day. She had her own prayer mat. She apparently would do this during her morning and afternoon break, and during lunch. There was not enough room around her desk to kneel without blocking an aisle, or someone else's work area, so she had taken to using the women's room because of the privacy it offered.

What responsibilities did the manager have in this situation? Our friends, **Lydia** and **Wes** discuss the options:

Lydia: Well, this may be an isolated incident, but our community has increasing numbers of people who immigrated, or whose families immigrated, from parts of the world where religious practices that may be unusual to us are indeed common throughout the culture. The law gives you a broad degree of latitude in deciding how to accommodate a difference in religion. It would seem to be practical to consider as a factor how many of these situations might arise.

Wes: You mean, if we make an accommodation in her case, then are we going to have to make the same accommodation in dozens of other cases?

Lydia: That's one way of looking at it, I suppose. But, I think you can turn that around, too. If there are dozens of employees in our workforce who want to be able to go somewhere and pray during the day, then — well, what I'm saying is that at some point if it appears that this is an issue which affects a lot of people, we may want that fact to weigh *in favor* of working something out to accommodate her, rather than simply rejecting accommodation as being too much of a hassle.

Wes: What is a reasonable solution, here? And, what are we saying about the role of diversity management here?

Lydia: I suppose it's tempting to suggest that it's up to the manager of that department to learn a little bit more about that religion, or the culture surrounding that religion. But, what about that? Is it reasonable to expect our managers to become experts in all the different cultures and religions that they might encounter?

Wes: There's a lot we expect them to know already. It seems that maybe a better expectation — or a more reasonable expectation — would be simply to ask that our managers be sensitive to situations like this, and be able to handle the situation without offending anyone's personal beliefs, and to work out a solution that treats this issue with the respect that it deserves, while not interfering with basic workplace access. After all, I think that's what most employees would expect as well. If there was some isolated spot we could let her use for the time being, I would be inclined to make an arrangement, so long as it was explained to her that we could not guarantee that such an arrangement would always be possible.

Lydia: That's probably more than we would actually be required to do under the law, but — again — this is a solution that recognizes an individual difference in a manner that is not contrary to the law.

Wes: Okay, there is a second situation I'd like your thoughts on. It arose at our customer service counter at one of our locations. It is in the West in a community that has attracted a lot of immigrants and refugees from Southeast Asia. As the population mix in that particular community has changed, so has the mix of people coming into our service facility. One day, a woman came in who wanted assistance with a problem. But she did not speak English. Our manager, almost instinctively, went to one of his employees who had come to this country from Southeast Asia who speaks English very well. He asked her to translate, so that the customer could be helped. Our employee responded without any objection, helped our service reps understand what the customer's problem was, and then translated the advice from our technical people so the customer knew what to do. It all seemed to work out very well.

Lydia: It doesn't sound like a problem.

Wes: Well, the situation has re-occurred. It is no longer unusual for someone who speaks no English to come in for assistance. In fact, the manager thinks our willingness to work with the folks who speak little or no English has helped our reputation in that community. But, the manager now has learned through the grapevine that our "employee-translator" has been having to work through her lunch hour and her breaks in order to get her own work done, because she is being asked so often to serve as a translator.

Lydia: Has she gone to the manager to complain?

Wes: No, apparently because she does not want him to think she is unwilling to do whatever is required. And she feels it is important for someone to be able to help these customers. After all, she is a part of the same community.

Lydia: So, what we're seeing is a situation where the manager gave someone "extra" duties without formally changing the job, and he just assumes that when employees have a problem they are going to come to him and say something. How is he supposed to know that she has this heavy burden if she doesn't say anything?

Wes: How is the employee supposed to know it is okay for her to say something unless the manager gives her the opportunity? Admittedly, there are two places we can put the blame for this lack of communication. But, I think the responsibility for solving it is with our manager. Again, the problem seems to be that we tend to assume that everyone is going to know about, and immediately be comfortable with, our custom of simply speaking up when things are not okay.

Lydia: So, are we saying that because this woman is from another country, the manager should have given her special attention; that when he gives her work, he should go out of his way more than he would with other people to let her know that he wants feedback to know how much of a burden this is creating?

Wes: I guess I'm saying that he should be doing that, yes. Not because this particular woman is from another country, but because she — as an *individual* — seems to be someone who is reluctant to speak up. Perhaps this reluctance is because she was taught that certain behavior is appropriate, that the boss is due a certain deference or that a worker shouldn't question assignments.

Lydia: Well, I don't know if this kind of reticence is more common in some cultures than others — and I really don't care. The point is, there are *individuals* from all cultures who are reticent, and to be most effective as a manager, our manager needs to be able to communicate effectively with these individuals. Simply because he is managing a diverse group of people, he should make special efforts to make sure everyone understands the rules and the accepted procedures.

Wes: And, maybe this is one of those situations where even the "accepted procedures" need to be re-examined.

Lydia: I don't know exactly how things are handled at that office, but if we have a changing workforce, with people from various backgrounds, maybe it becomes more important for the manager to have more individual contact with employees, on a routine basis, just to assure that everyone has had the chance to become comfortable with the idea of talking to him about the work, or about a problem.

Wes: One of the points made by a number of the diversity consultants is the difficulty folks can have playing the game when they don't know the rules. Or when they think they understand the rules, but they really don't understand as many of the rules as the other people who are playing the game. I went through one session where we played a game at our table, and some people were told all of the rules, and some people were told only some of the rules. It can be very frustrating, especially when you are taking "the game" seriously, to find out at the end that your efforts were undercut by the fact that you were working with an incomplete, or inaccurate, set of rules.

Lydia: I guess we're all learning from this process.

Commentary

The types of issues being discussed above are typical of the situations that arise as managers encounter an increasingly diverse workforce. A sound approach to such situations must begin with a clear understanding of the employer's basic obligations under the law.

The fact that a person comes from a different background, has religious practices we are unfamiliar with, or speaks with an accent is not a legitimate reason for excluding that person from our workplace. And once that person is employed, such facts should not be a reason for treating this person differently. At the same time, when we assess the person, we may find that he or she — as an individual who comes from a different background — faces certain hurdles that did not exist or which were not so evident in the context of a more homogenous workforce. We may also find that, because of his or her different background this individual brings to our workplace certain positive attributes that were missing or were not evident in a more homogenous workforce.

The question for us, as employers or managers, is how much are we willing to do to eliminate or minimize those hurdles in order to get the benefit of this individual as a productive employee. In some instances, the answer to this question may be found through a simple cost/benefit analysis. To do that analysis, however, a manager must be sensitive to the nature of the potential hurdles; otherwise, in our increasingly diverse workforce, the manager will simply watch as one employee after another comes into the workplace and fails or leaves without reaching his or her potential. Moreover, to do that cost/benefit analysis accurately, the manager needs to be sensitive to the contribution a person with a different background and a different perspective may bring to the workplace. Otherwise, the manager may never see the economic wisdom of investing in the elimination of those hurdles.

CHAPTER X

CONCLUSION

For companies and managers looking to the future, a very simple but very critical question is: "Where are we going to get the people we need to do the work?" Considering the pressure to produce quality products and the escalating skill requirements for the jobs of today and tomorrow, it becomes clear that competitiveness will be tied to the ability to attract and retain skilled workers. The response to this realization for a variety of employers has been to take steps to assure that their workplace provides an environment that respects and accommodates the many individual differences that skilled workers bring with them to the job.

To be sure, not every employer's initiative in this area is the same. But for the most part, each initiative has focused on promoting sound management skills, combined with a sensitivity for the differences in individuals. Each initiative has reflected a willingness to re-examine various practices and policies, and each initiative has reflected the importance of the manager's role in promoting an environment that takes a more inclusive and less exclusive approach to individual differences. At the same time, these initiatives have stressed the importance of a core set of values — most often including an emphasis on quality — that can serve to bring individuals together as a productive team. To make these initiatives successful, it has been important to recognize the relationship between the principles of our EEO laws and the concept of diversity management.

Today we can observe that the way employers have responded to the EEO laws has been to develop consistent, job-related standards and practices that ultimately assure an increased measure of fairness to *all* employees. A diversity management initiative, carefully planned and soundly implemented, can assist an employer's voluntary efforts to move further in that direction.

The changing demographics and the changing business environment will present a variety of challenges. Some of those challenges we can anticipate; others we may not have the same opportunity to prepare for. In either situation, the principles of equal employment opportunity — with their focus on the individual — can provide a sound approach for managers as they seek to respond to these challenges. Indeed, for those workers who find themselves in a workplace populated with people of many different backgrounds, the promise of equal opportunity will be as important as ever.

RESOURCES

There is a broad range of resources available to assist an employer in developing a greater awareness and appreciation of individual differences, and the skills needed to manage a diverse workforce. Most companies have found it useful to draw upon a variety of resources to fashion a diversity initiative that responds to their particular needs.

Among the best known resources is the "Valuing Diversity" series of seven films produced by Copeland Griggs Productions in San Francisco, California. Also, BNAC Communications of Rockville, Maryland, has produced a popular video training program, "Bridges: Skills for Managing a Diverse Workforce."

In considering the relationship between diversity management and the law regarding EEO and affirmative action, an article that may be of interest is: R. Roosevelt Thomas, Jr., *From Affirmative Action to Affirming Diversity,* Harvard Business Review, March - April 1990, at 107.

There are any number of experts available to assist an employer in developing a greater awareness and appreciation of cultural and other differences among employees. There is also a considerable amount of literature that can assist in the broadening process. For example, with respect to some of the specific concerns mentioned in Chapter V, "Understanding Differences," you might consult *Black Life in Corporate America: Swimming in the Mainstream* by George Davis and Glegg Watson (Anchor Press, 1982); *The Black*

Manager: Making It In The Corporate World, by Floyd Dickens, Jr. and Jacqueline B. Dickens (AMACOM, 1982); and *Black Managers: The Dream Deferred,* by Edward W. Jones, Jr., in Harvard Business Review, May-June 1986, at 84.

In addition, for a more general description of the dilemma faced by persons who are seen not as individuals but only as a member of a different race, see *Invisible Man* by Ralph Ellison (Random House, 1952). A variety of literature, although not quite as extensive, also exists with respect to individuals from other racial and ethnic groups. See, for example, *The Minority Executives' Handbook,* by Randolph W. Cameron (Warner Books, 1989). In addition, much has been written about the barriers faced by women who enter jobs in what had been predominantly or exclusively a male world. See, for example, *Breaking the Glass Ceiling: Can Women Make It to the Top in America's Largest Corporations?* by Ann M. Morrison (Addison-Wesley, 1987).

The successful management of diversity in the workplace is essentially an extension of traditional good management skills. There are a number of sources which deal with these "people skills," including the following, each of which received the annual book award from the Society for Human Resources Management (formerly the American Society for Personnel Administration):

S. Smith and B. Olmsted, *Creating a Flexible Workplace* (AMACOM 1989);

M. London, *Changing Agents: New Roles and Innovation Strategies for Human Resource Professionals* (Jossey-Bass Publishing Co. 1988);

P. Block, *The Empowered Manager: Positive Political Skills at Work* (Jossey-Bass Publishing Co. 1987);

D. Kirkpatrick, *How To Manage Change Effectively* (Jossey-Bass Publishing Co. 1985);

R. Henderson, *Practical Guide To Performance Appraisal* (Reston Publishing Co. 1984);

D. L. Bradford and A. R. Cohen, *Managing for Excellence* (Wiley, 1984); and

D. Kirkpatrick, *How To Improve Performance Through Appraisal and Coaching* (AMACOM, 1982).

Some other useful resources include:

Managing a Diverse Workforce: How to Deal with Value Conflicts, Trainer's Workshop (American Management Association, December 1987).

V. L. Tyler, *Intercultural Interacting,* David M. Kennedy Center for International Studies (Brigham Young University, 1987).

L. Martel, *Mastering Change* (Simon & Schuster, 1986)

For those who wish to read about initiatives by particular companies, the following articles may be of interest:

G. Haight, *Managing Diversity,* Across the Board, March 1990, at 22.

L. Copeland, *Valuing Diversity, Part I: Making the Most of Cultural Differences at the Workplace,* Personnel, June 1988, at 52.

L. Copeland, *Valuing Diversity, Part II: Pioneers and Champions of Change,* Personnel, July 1988, at 44.

D. Maraniss, *Firm Makes Racial Revolution From Top Down,* The Washington Post, March 8, 1990, at A1.

J. Schachter, *Firms Begin to Embrace Diversity,* Los Angeles Times, April 17, 1988, at 1.

S. Nelton, *Meet Your New Work Force,* Nation's Business, July 1988, at 14.

THE FOUNDATION' S TRAINING MANUALS

Basic EEO Resource Manual by Douglas S. McDowell, Jeffrey A. Norris and Lorence L. Kessler, 800 pp. paper (1990) $275.00 per set

Developing Effective Affirmative Action Plans by Jeffrey A. Norris and Salvador T. Perkins, 632 pp. paper (1990) $125.00

Effective Handling Of EEO Charges: A Guide For Employers by Robert E. Williams and Salvador T. Perkins, 248 pp. paper (1990) $50.00

Statistics For Non-Statisticians: A Primer For Professionals by Farrell Bloch, 188 pp. paper (1987) $25.00

Equity At Work: A Manager's Guide To Fair Employment Laws And Practices by Robert E. Williams and Jeffrey A. Norris, 98 pp. paper (1990) $35.00

For information about the Foundation's training manuals call (202) 789-8685 or write to the Foundation at the address given on the opposite page.